# Stern's Guide To
# Disney
# Collectibles

MICKEY MOUSE TARGET

D1385006

# Stern's Guide To
# Disney Collectibles

## Michael Stern

**COLLECTOR BOOKS**
*A Division of Schroeder Publishing Co., Inc.*

The current values in this book should be used only as a guide. They are not intended to set prices, which vary from one section of the country to another. Auction prices as well as dealer prices vary greatly and are affected by condition as well as demand. Neither the Author nor the Publisher assumes responsibility for any losses that might be incurred as a result of consulting this guide.

The prices in this guide are derived by the author, wholly independent of The Walt Disney Company and The Walt Disney Company has no connection therewith.

This book makes reference to "Mickey Mouse" and other various characters and films produced by The Walt Disney Company. All of the Disney characters and films are copyrighted by The Walt Disney Company. The characters also serve as trademarks of The Walt Disney Company.

Additional copies of this book may be ordered from

COLLECTOR BOOKS
P.O. Box 3009
Paducah, Kentucky  42002-3009

@ $14.95. Add $2.00 for postage and handling.

Copyright: Michael Stern, 1989
Values Updated: 1992

This book or any part thereof may not be reproduced without the written consent of the Author and Publisher.

Printed in Hong Kong by Everbest Printing through Four Colour Imports, Ltd.

# Dedication

This book is dedicated to all those Disneyana collectors who share the same excitement and joy I do when finding that incredible piece to add to their collection.

# Record Prices

Phillips Toy Auction held in New York on October 10, 1987 set records for the sale of many toys. "A rare early mechanical Japanese celluloid figure of Mickey Mouse went for $4,400.00. This piece went without the box and was not in mint condition as is this one.

# Contents

# Acknowledgments

To my wife Merrill who puts up with my Disney craziness and designed my "Mickey" room where I display all my treasures.

To my twin daughters, Jenny and Lisa, who are now five years old and have ventured out with me to flea markets and antique stores since they were two, spotting a Disney piece and screaming, "Daddy there's a Mickey!"

To Jim and Melissa, my cohorts, in the collecting of Disneyana and to Lee and Young whose photography is truly a work of art.

And to all those super people out there who I've bought from, sold to and traded with; without whom this book could not have been written.

# Introduction

There's no greater thrill than to find a Disneyana collectible not previously seen before. All collectors of Disneyana memorabilia share the dream of finding those incredibly unusual and rare pieces. The fact is that though it is a rare occasion, there are literally thousands of Disney collectibles hidden and stored in people's attics and basements waiting to be rediscovered.

The largest comic-character collectible field today is that of Disneyana. Mickey Mouse and his friends are the most sought after because everyone of every age and nationality identifies with them. Their popularity continues to grow at a tremendous rate among nostalgia collectors, far surpassing that of other comic characters—Felix, Popeye, and Little Orphan Annie.

Throughout the years, Disney merchandise has been mass produced and mass marketed; so through the years, many items have been put away, forgotten, and left to be found years later by unsuspecting relatives or garage sale groupies. Every year more and more exciting Disneyana collectibles are uncovered, and they slip into the market place waiting to be gobbled up by Mickey Mouse fanatics who live and breathe for that new piece to add to their collection. Many collectors can relate to these pieces because they are part of their past. As children, these were the toys they played with, the clothes they wore, the toothbrush holders they used nightly, and the wrist watches they wore daily.

The fervor of collecting Disneyana is unique in its intensity as Disney enthusiasts venture to garage sales, antique stores and flea markets in search of these treasures of the past. These relics are out there and can be reasonably purchased. Many collectors go to toy and doll shows and wait in line for hours before the show begins so as to be the first ones through the turnstiles and the first to see and be able to purchase the Disney collectibles they hope they will find. Many "Mickey Mouse fanatics" subscribe to the various toy magazines and participate in auctions that employ mail and phone bidding. Some, like myself, are members of the Mouse Club, which caters solely to collectors of Disneyana. Many attend their annual Disneyana collectors convention in Anaheim, California.

All of the photographs in this book are taken from my personal collection. I have been collecting for only three years. It took a lot of leg work, a multitude of patience, and a lot of luck—being in the right place at the right time. The five celluloid Mickeys pictured at the beginning of this introduction was purchased from an ad in the "Antique Trader" for $55.00. The gentleman I purchased it from had found it in an elderly lady's attic as he was rummaging around during a garage sale. The salient point is that all of the photographs in this book are of Disneyana that I recently acquired. The reality is that these artifacts of the past are out there today in the hundreds and even thousands. They do exist and can be found by today's collectors.

I have seen Disney World and Disneyland memorabilia for sale at flea markets priced higher than they are currently selling for in the theme park gift shops and have seen unusual 1930's Disneyana toys at ridiculously low prices. My hope is that this book will assist one who finds a piece of Disney memorabilia in dating it and putting its price into perspective.

# Pie-eyed Mickey and Minnie

Mickey Mouse was created in 1928, and since his inception, has been the backbone of the Disney dynasty. Since Steamboat Willie, his first cartoon, was released on November 18, 1928, Mickey Mouse became an immediate and unqualified success. Mickey Mouse may be the most recognized and perfect graphic symbol of any cartoon character ever created. He is the most sought after in the nostalgia market place and is the superstar of all Disneyana collectibles. Mickey and Minnie Mouse memorabilia became pop culture artifacts.

This chapter is entitled "Pie-Eyed Mickey and Minnie," and all items pictured are from the years 1928-1938. This is the period from which sophisticated Mickey Mouse memorabiliacs feel produced the finest and most valuable collector's items. Many sophisticated collectors seek only items manufactured from these "golden" years. Mickey Mouse and Minnie Mouse from this period were created as primitive and impish rodents and are most recognizable by their pie shaped eyes. The eyes look as though a sliver of pie has been removed from them leaving a blank indentation.

Mickey and Minnie of the 1930's have the look of a happy rodent with a pot belly; a thin, long, string, mouse-like tail; stove pipe arms and legs; overly large, bulbous shoes; two button shorts; thick, four-finger, glove-like hands and black balloon ears.

Walt Disney described his early Mouse: "His head is a circle with an oblong circle for a snout. The ears are also circles so they can be drawn the same, no matter how he turns his head. His body is like a pear with a long tail."

Early Mickey and Minnie are in direct contrast to their latter day counter-parts who are pink faced, more humanoid, and minus the tail. The pie eyes were filled with black circles. Through the years, Mickey also shed his pot belly.

The various items of the 1930's are distinguishable by their markings. Usually, these items are marked "Walter E. Disney," "Walt Disney," or Walt Disney Enterprises. On occasion, just the initials "W.D.E." were utilized. Some items were manufactured with stick-on labels or import stamps that through the years have fallen off or been removed.

Pie-eyed Mickey was featured in every imaginable type of toy and household item. Items that carried his image became overnight best sellers. Mickey and Minnie were constant house guests, and it was rare indeed to go through a normal day without being influenced by Disney's Mouse.

In Cecil Munsey's book, *Disneyana*, he quotes a writer in 1935 describing the tremendous presence of Mickey Mouse. As that writer put it:

Shoppers carry Mickey satchels and briefcases bursting with Mickey Mouse soap, candy, playing cards, bridge favours, hair-brushes, chinaware, alarm clocks and hot-water bottles, wrapped in Mickey Mouse paper, tied with Mickey Mouse ribbon and paid for out of Mickey Mouse purses with savings hoarded in Mickey Mouse banks. At the lunch counter—Mickey Mouse table covers and napkins—they consume Mickey biscuits and dairy products while listening to Mickey Mouse music from Mickey Mouse phonographs and radios. Then, glancing at their Mickey Mouse wrist-watches, they dash away to buy Mickey Mouse toothbrushes—they wear Mickey Mouse caps, waists (shirts or blouses), socks, shoes, slippers, garters, mittens, aprons, bibs and underthings, and beneath Mickey Mouse rain-capes and umbrellas they go to school where Mickey Mouse desk outfits turn lessons into pleasure. They play with Mickey Mouse velocipedes (tricycles), footballs, baseballs, bounce-balls, bats, catching gloves, doll houses, doll dishes, tops, blocks, drums, puzzles, games—paint sets, sewing sets, drawing sets, stamping sets, jack sets, bubble sets, pull toys, push toys, animated toys, tents, camp stools, sand pails, masks, blackboards, and balloons—until day is done, when they sup from Mickey Mouse cups, porringers (bowls) and baby plates and lie down to sleep in Mickey Mouse pajamas between Mickey Mouse crib

sheets, to waken in the morn smiling at Mickey Mouse pictures on the nursery walls covered with Mickey Mouse wallpaper.

The pictorial section on Pie-Eyed Mickey opens up with an extremely rare toy. Shown with its original box in *Plate 1* is Rambling Mickey Mouse, a celluloid wind up that graphically shows an early pie-eyed Mickey. The use of celluloid revolutionized the toy industry as it allowed the manufacturer to reproduce minute detail in vibrant color. This piece is an excellent example of celluloid use. It is rare to find a piece where the celluloid has remained flawless. Many pieces experienced dents because of the thin nature of the material that was easily crushed by children. The Rambling Mickey's tail is steel and was used to add balance as Mickey moved forward. The piece was copyrighted in 1934 and distributed by the George Borgfeldt Corporation. The original sticker is found under the left shoe. The box has the original price tag from Leonard Brothers department store and sold for $.49.

Another unusual celluloid toy also shown with its original box in *Plate 2* is Mickey and Minnie Acrobats. As a result of the durability and lightweight of celluloid, these figures twirl and flip after being wound up. This was a Nifty toy distributed by Borgfeldt and both Mickey and Minnie were marked "WALT E. DISNEY" on their necks. An interesting fact about this particular toy is that all known examples have noses that are pushed inwards because the box that they were sold in was made too small.

Many Mickey toys gained overnight success and had a major impact on the companies that manufactured them. A perfect example is the Mickey and Minnie Handcar in *Plate 3* that saved the Lionel Train Company from bankruptcy. This toy was first produced in May 1934 for that year's Christmas market. Orders exceeded 350,000 and at $1.00 a piece overnight Lionel's fortunes were reversed. The idea of Mickey and Minnie pumping away caught the public's fancy. Even though Lionel's factory was in production seven days and seven nights a week, demand could not be met.

Another real success story of Disney merchandising is with the Ingersoll Waterbury Company. In 1933, they too were on the verge of bankruptcy when a deal was struck to produce Mickey Mouse watches. The first two are pictured in *Plate 4 and 5*. Macy's department store in New York sold 11,000 in one day. In eight weeks, to keep up with the barrage of orders, Ingersoll had gone from 300 to 30,000 employees. In 1933, 900,000 were sold and by June of 1935, 2½ million watches had been purchased at a retail price of $2.95. Mickey's hands not only told time, but assumed hundreds of amusing positions. The second hand also had great Mickey graphics—four revolving Mickeys. Both watches have Mickey Mouse Ingersoll printed on the face. The metal link band is more preferable to collectors than the leather band with two enamel Mickeys.

Kay Kamen, the man behind early Disney merchandising, established strong connections with Japanese toy makers, and this resulted in the mass production of bisque figurines. The cheap labor in Japan enabled these very collectible figurines to be hand painted and thus show fine detail. These were made in various sizes. The largest, and only 9½" bisque, is of Mickey and is pictured in *Plate 6*. This is the rarest of all Disney bisques. Not only is the size unique, but both arms are movable.

The most valuable and highly sought after bisque figurines are those with movable arms; especially the ones used as toothbrush holders.

*Plates 7, 8, 9 and 10* show four of the six different Mickey and Minnie movable arm toothbrush holders. In *Plates 8 and 9* both the heads are oversized and are referred to as "bulbous" heads. They all have indentations where the toothbrush could rest upon and the handle of the brush would fit in the curved arm of the figure.

Serious Disneyana collectors are always in search of boxed bisque sets. Most people, as is the case today, discarded the boxes when they opened the toys. The boxed bisque set in *Plate 12* is The Three Pals featuring Mickey, Minnie and Pluto. This set has the original import sticker and was copyrighted in 1930 and distributed by the George Borgfeldt Company. It is marked "WALT DISNEY ENTERPRISES LIMITED." The original price tag is on the box. The set was sold at Rich's Department Store in Atlanta, Georgia, for $1.50.

Items manufactured in England are also highly sought after. The Mickey Mouse Post Office Bank in *Plate 11* was made in England by the Happynak Company. English products frequently were licensed separately. The bank is marked "BY PERMISSION OF WALT DISNEY MICKEY MOUSE LT HAPPYNAK SERIES MADE IN GREAT BRITAIN".

Mickey and Minnie were used on imaginary and real dining tables throughout the 1930's. High quality lusterware china tea sets, like those pictured in *Plate 13 and Plate 14* were mass produced in Japan. Usually only the bigger pieces (tea cup, sugar dish, creamer) were marked "W.D.E." the others (saucers, cups and plates) have just "Japan" on the bottoms.

One of the rarest pieces in the book is the largest version of the Fun-E-Flex wood and composition figure pictured in Plate 15. Mickey is 9¼" high and has a cloth covered wire tail which has a wooden knob on the end. The body is jointed and fully flexible and the head is composition while the rest of the body is wood. Mickey has "lollipop" hands. This toy was also made in red and yellow.

The porcelain-clad metal child's potty in *Plate 16* was made in Germany by the Richard G. Krueger Company. The graphics on the front are extremely bright and colorful.

It was not unusual to enhance the value of a wind up toy by adding a celluloid Mickey or Minnie. Such is the case in *Plate 17* of Mickey on an early wind up rocking horse. The rocking horse moves back and forth with Mickey along for the ride. The horse is made of wood and hand painted so that the details are fine.

Many Mickey Mouse items served dual purposes like the jam jar bank produced by Glaser Crandell Company of Chicago in *Plate 18*. After the jam was consumed the jar became a coin bank. Mickey Mouse, Minnie Mouse, Horace Horsecollar and Clarabelle the Cow were embossed in glass around the jar. The top of the jar has a coin slot and a picture of Mickey's head with the saying "Feed Mickey For Wealth Eat Jam for Health." The label that originally came with the jar is hard to come by and when the piece has it the value is greatly enhanced.

One of the earliest companies to manufacture Mickey Mouse dolls was the Margarete Steiff Company which still produces dolls today. The Steiff Mickey Mouse hand puppet in *Plate 19* has the original button in his ear which is a trademark of all Steiff dolls. The original tag is also in place. The hand puppet is made of sateen and velvet material and wood pulp. The mouth is drawn on and the original string whiskers are included.

PLATE 1
RAMBLING MICKEY MOUSE is celluloid wind-up that was distributed in 1934 by the George Borgfeldt Company. The celluloid allowed the manufacturer to reproduce minute detail and vibrant color. The tail is steel to help with balance. Mickey is 7″ tall. A wind up mechanism is encased in his body.

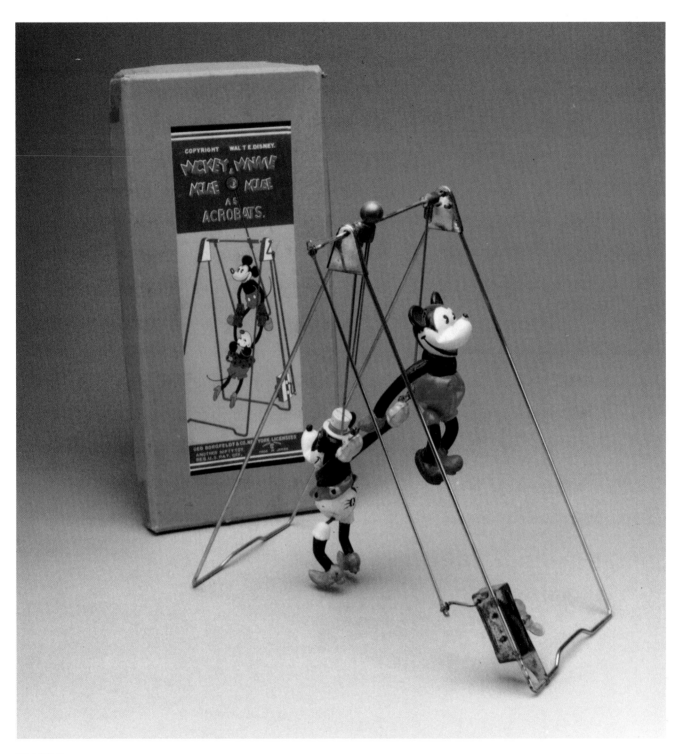

PLATE 2
MICKEY AND MINNIE ACROBATS were made by Nifty Toys in the 1930's. Mickey and Minnie are celluloid. When the piece is wound up, they spin and twirl. The noses are idented as the boxes they were sold in were made too small. They are marked on their necks, "WALT E DISNEY."

PLATE 3
LIONEL MICKEY AND MINNIE HANDCAR saved The Lionel Company from bankruptcy. It was first produced in May 1934. The body of the handcar is tin and is 8″ long and 6″ high. It came with 72″ of track. Mickey and Minnie's bodies are composition and their tails and legs are natural rubber. The handcar also came in green, orange and a very rare maroon.

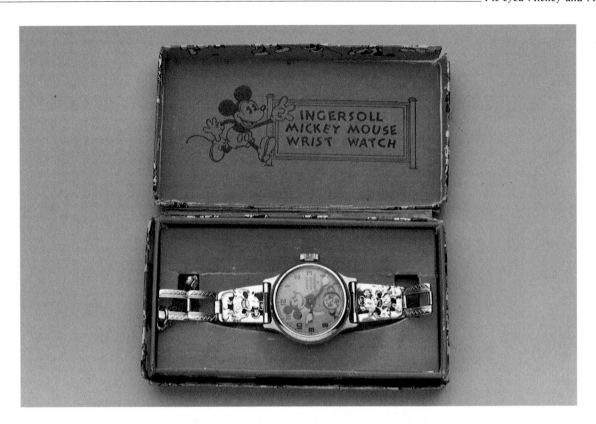

PLATE 4
MICKEY MOUSE WRIST WATCH was made by the Ingersoll Waterbury Company in 1933. This was the first Mickey Mouse wrist watch made. The band is metal with links and is highlighted on both sides by metal Mickeys. The second hand pictures four Mickeys and revolves. The retail price for this watch in 1935 was $2.95.

PLATE 5
MICKEY MOUSE WRIST WATCH. This is the other version of the Ingersoll wrist watch. The band is leather with two enamel Mickeys on each side. The original box is orange and featured the early Disney characters; Horace Horsecollar and Clarabelle the Cow. It retailed for $3.75 in 1933 and 1934.

PLATE 6
MICKEY MOUSE BISQUE. This is the largest Mickey Mouse bisque ever made. Mickey is 9½" tall and both arms are movable. The base in the front is marked "Mickey Mouse" and the back is marked "WALT E DISNEY." This is the rarest of all Disney bisques.

PLATE 7
MICKEY MOUSE BISQUE TOOTHBRUSH HOLDER was made in Japan and marked on his back "WALTER E DISNEY". Mickey is 5″ tall and one arm is movable. The toothbrush slides between the circular arm and rests in an indentation on the foot.

PLATE 8
MICKEY MOUSE BISQUE TOOTHBRUSH HOLDER. This toothbrush holder is noted for Mickey's head which is described as bulbous. This was hand painted in Japan and "MICKEY MOUSE" is inscribed across his stomach. Toothbrush holders with jointed movable arms are preferable to all others.

PLATE 9
MINNIE MOUSE BISQUE TOOTHBRUSH HOLDER is similar to Mickey in Plate 8 because of her bulbous head. The name "MINNIE MOUSE" is inscribed across her body and on the back it is marked "WALTER E DISNEY."

PLATE 10
MINNIE MOUSE BISQUE TOOTHBRUSH HOLDER also has the movable arm. The black elastic that holds the arm in place can clearly be seen. Minnie's head is tilted in comparison to Plate 9 where she looks straight ahead. These toothbrush holders are highly sought after by Disneyana collectors.

PLATE 11
MICKEY MOUSE POST OFFICE BANK was made in
England by the Happynak Company. There is a slit in the
side to deposit coins. The bank is marked "BY PERMIS-
SION OF WALT DISNEY MICKEY MOUSE LT. HAP-
PYNAK SERIES MADE IN GREAT BRITAIN."

PLATE 12
THE THREE PALS BISQUE SET was made and hand
painted in Japan and features Mickey, Minnie and Pluto.
To find a set in a box is very rare and the value is increas-
ed greatly. The paper label is on Mickey's left foot and
is marked "WALT DISNEY ENTERPRISES,
COPYRIGHT 1930." Mickey and Minnie are 5″ tall and
Pluto is 4½″ tall.

PLATE 13
MICKEY MOUSE AND MINNIE MOUSE CERAMIC LUSTERWARE TEA SET. This beautiful set was made in Japan. The tea pot and sugar dish are marked "WALT E DISNEY MADE IN JAPAN." The cups and saucers are just marked "JAPAN." To find a complete boxed set is unusual.

PLATE 14
MICKEY AND MINNIE CERAMIC LUSTERWARE TEA SET is very similar to Plate 13 except a blue color was used to highlight each piece. Children in the 1930's used these sets for their imaginary tea parties. Note the graphics on each differ from each other as many different sets were manufactured with various scenes.

PLATE 15
FUN E FLEX WOOD AND COMPOSITION MICKEY MOUSE. This toy is one of the rarest in the book. It is the largest (9¼" high) of the wooden body, composition head, Fun E Flex Mickey Mouse's. The wire tail is cloth covered and the body is jointed and fully flexible. The hands are referred to as "lollipop" because of their unusual shape.

**PLATE 16**
MICKEY MOUSE CHILD'S POTTY
is porcelain-clad metal made in Germany by the Richard G. Krueger Company. The colorful picture of Mickey and Minnie on the piano is on the outside of the potty.

**PLATE 17**
ROCKING HORSE MICKEY MOUSE
is one of the few hand painted wooden wind-up toys featuring Mickey Mouse that was produced in 1930's. Mickey Mouse is made of celluloid and the horse and base are made of wood. When the toy is wound up the horse rocks back and forth utilizing a very simple wind-up mechanism.

**PLATE 18**
MICKEY MOUSE JAM JAR BANK was
manufactured by the Glaser Crandell Company of Chicago. The container served a dual
purpose—jam was actually sold in the jar and
when emptied it became a bank. Mickey
Mouse, Minnie Mouse and Horace
Horsecollar are embossed in the glass. The
top of the jar has Mickey's head and the saying "FEED MICKEY WEALTH, EAT JAM
FOR HEALTH." If found with the original
jam label, it is more valuable.

**PLATE 19**
MICKEY MOUSE STEIFF HAND PUPPET
was made in Germany by the Margarete Steiff
Company which still produces dolls today.
The puppet is made of sateen and velvet
material and wood pulp. The original Steiff
button is in Mickey's car and the original tag
that says "MICKEY MOUSE c WALT
DISNEY" is in place. The mouth is drawn
on and the whiskers are made of string.

PLATE 20
MICKEY MOUSE CHILD'S TELEPHONE was made by N.N. Hill Brass Company. A cardboard Mickey Mouse grins at you as you dial your number and the bell rings. The mouth piece, the receiver and the hook are nickel plated. The base is enameled metal. The receiver is made of wood. The phone is 8″ high. It is marked "c WALT DISNEY."

PLATE 21
MICKEY MOUSE DOLLHOUSE was made by the O.B. Andrews Company of Chattanooga, Tennessee. It is made of fiber board and comes in three sizes; this one being the smallest. It measures 14″ wide by 10″ high.

PLATE 22
MICKEY MOUSE AND MINNIE
MOUSE MUSICIAN BISQUES. This
is a collection of Mickey Mouse bisques all carrying or playing a musical
instrument that were made and hand
painted in Japan and imported by
George Borgfeldt Company. All are
marked ''c WALT E DISNEY.''

PLATE 23
MICKEY MOUSE AND MINNIE
MOUSE GLASS TUMBLERS were
made in 1938 by the Libbey Glass
Company of Toledo, Ohio. Character
glasses were very popular in the
1930's. Both glasses are marked
''W.D.''

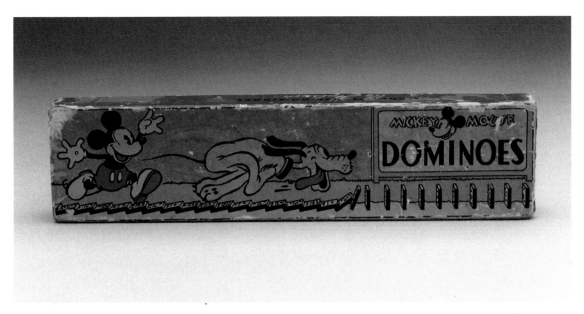

PLATE 24
MICKEY MOUSE DOMINOES were made by the Halsam Company and licensed by Walt Disney Enterprises. The dominoes are solid black with no pictorials of any kind.

PLATE 25
MICKEY MOUSE LUSTERWARE ASHTRAY. Mickey is playing a drum in this version. The ashtray has been glazed and is ceramic and marked on the bottom "MADE IN JAPAN."

PLATE 26
MICKEY MOUSE AND MINNIE MOUSE BISQUE
TOOTHBRUSH HOLDER is hand painted and made in
Japan. There are two square holes in the back of the piece
that can hold two toothbrushes. It is marked "WALT E
DISNEY."

PLATE 27
*Item A*: LARGE RUBBER MICKEY MOUSE made by the
Seiberling Latex Products Company of Akron, Ohio.
Mickey is solid rubber and is 6″ tall. The head is movable.
This version is much harder to find. *Item B*: SMALL RUB-
BER MICKEY MOUSE also made by Seiberling Latex Pro-
ducts Company is solid rubber. This Mickey, which stands
up easier than the larger version, is 3½″. It originally sold
for 39¢.

PLATE 28
**MICKEY MOUSE TARGET** is from the 1934 Mickey Mouse target game made by The Marks Brothers Company of Boston. This set came with tripod, six rubber filled vacuum cup darts and an enameled steel gun with powerful spring. The Mickey Mouse in the target is a good graphic of a 1930's pie-eyed Mickey.

**PLATE 29**
MINNIE MOUSE CELLULOID NURSERY DOLL made in Japan is 5″ tall and has two movable arms. The head is referred to as bulbous, oversized in comparison to the body.

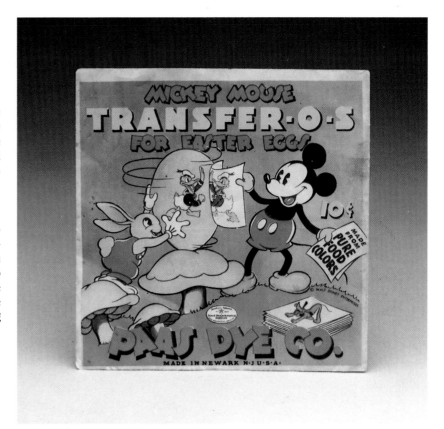

PLATE 30
MICKEY MOUSE TRANSFER-O-S was made by the Paas Dye Company of Newark, New Jersey and was used to decorate Easter eggs. They are made from pure food colors and had the Good Housekeeping seal of approval. They are marked "WALT DISNEY ENTERPRISES."

PLATE 31
MICKEY MOUSE PRINT SHOP was manufactured in the U.S.A. by the Fulton Specialty Company as part of their Fulton Faultless Education Toy line. It came with a stamp pad, rubber stamp letters and rubber picture stamps. It also came with small metal tweezers. The Mickey Mouse Print Shop came in three sizes; this one being the middle size.

PLATE 32
MICKEY MOUSE AND MINNIE MOUSE NEEDLECRAFT PILLOWCASE made by Vogue Needlecraft in 1931.
These pieces are marked "WALT DISNEY PRODUCTIONS" even though made in the 1930's.

PLATE 33
MINNIE MOUSE CHINA MUG made by the Patriot China Company is 4″ tall. Horace Horsecollar, an early
Disney character, is pictured on the back. The piece is signed "WALT DISNEY."

PLATE 34
MICKEY MOUSE FIGURAL SOAP was made by the Castille Soap Company and the set was manufactured by Weco Products Company. It is rare to find a soap that has lasted because of the brittle nature of the product. The colorful box is also much sought after by collectors.

PLATE 35
*Item A*: MICKEY MOUSE TREASURE ISLAND SAND PAIL was made by The Happynak Company of Great Britian. "BY PERMISSION OF WALT DISNEY MICKEY MOUSE LTD," is printed on the sand pail. *Item B*: MICKEY MOUSE BEACH BAG. Mickey Mouse is silkscreened onto the beach bag. It is marked "W.D. ENT."

PLATE 36
MICKEY MOUSE HOOP-LA-GAME was made by the Marks Brothers Company. It was the earliest version of any Disney ring toss game. The hoops are made of wood. The game is marked "WALT DISNEY."

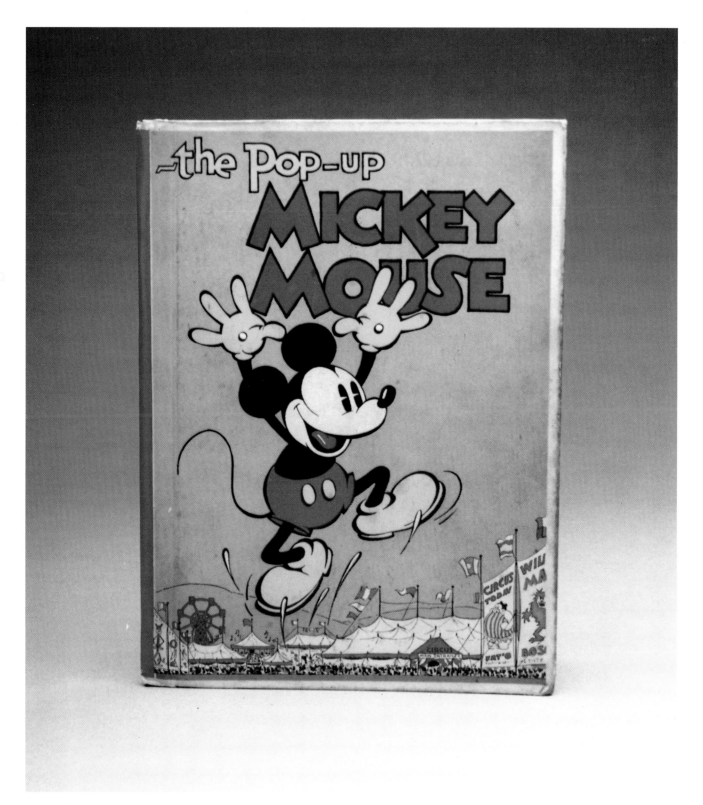

PLATE 37
MICKEY MOUSE POP-UP BOOK was published by the Blue Ribbon Books, Inc. of New York. The book is copyright 1933 by Walt Disney Enterprises. In this pop up book there are three beautifully graphic pop-up scenes.

PLATE 38
POP-UP SCENE FROM MICKEY MOUSE POP-UP BOOK. This is the center pop-up of the book. Mickey Mouse, Pluto and Pluto's dog house pop up from the page.

PLATE 39
MICKEY MOUSE KNICKERBOCKER DOLL was made by the Knickerbocker Doll Company in 1936. Mickey Mouse has tufted chaps that held two guns. The orange shoes are composition. This doll is referred to as two-gun Mickey. The original also had a cowboy hat and one hand held a lasso.

PLATE 40
MICKEY MOUSE DRUM was made by the Noble and Cooley Company. The drum is made of metal and is marked "C.W.D. ENT."

**PLATE 41**
MICKEY MOUSE LOOK ALIKE PIN CUSHIONS were produced in the millions in Japan in the 1930's. They are made of porcelain and were not licensed by Disney. Mickey Mouse knick-knacks, planters and ashtrays were produced as knock offs. They are also considered by some as collectibles. They are marked "JAPAN."

**PLATE 42**
MICKEY MOUSE, MINNIE MOUSE AND PLUTO BISQUE TOOTHBRUSH HOLDER was made in Japan. There are two holes in back of Mickey and Minnie's heads for toothbrushes. It is marked "WALT E DISNEY" on the back.

PLATE 43
*Item A*: MICKEY MOUSE HAIR BRUSH was made by the Henry L. Hughes Company of New York and sold for 59¢. It is made of wood with an ebony finish and a strip of red enamel. This piece is marked "W.D.E." *Item B*: MICKEY MOUSE BAR SOAP with transfer pictures were made by Pictorial Products, Inc. The Mickey Mouse toilet soap and colorful box is also sought after by collectors. The picture transfers are of Mickey Mouse, Minnie Mouse and Horace Horsecollar.

PLATE 44
MICKEY MOUSE SILVER SPOON was manufactured by William Rogers & Son. These were popular baby gifts. The Mickey Mouse spoon is silver plated.

PLATE 45
*Item A*: MICKEY MOUSE CELLULOID BABY RATTLE was made by the Amloid Company. It is 9″ tall. There are no markings. *Item B*:
MICKEY MOUSE CELLULOID BABY RATTLE is extremely rare. It was used as a Christmas toy and licensed by Walt Disney. The colors
were formed by separate pieces of tinted celluloid. This brilliance is not seen in typical Disney celluloid pieces. It was made in Japan in 1934.

PLATE 46
MICKEY AND MINNIE MOUSE CARPET SWEEPER was made by The Ohio Art Company in 1936. This child's toy is made of tin and is beautifully lithographed. The wheels and handle are made of wood. It is marked "c WALT DISNEY."

PLATE 47
WOODEN MICKEY FIGURE was a Fun-E-Flex product made in Japan and imported by the George Borgfeldt Company. This figure is 6½" tall and is recognizable by Mickey's lollipop hands, which with its larger size, makes this wooden piece very rare. It is marked "MICKEY MOUSE BY WALT DISNEY."

PLATE 48
MICKEY MOUSE FILM. This is an early Mickey Mouse Silly Symphony cartoon. It is marked "c WALT DISNEY ENTERPRISES."

PLATE 49
MICKEY AND MINNIE MOUSE BISQUE FIGURES were made in Japan and hand painted. Mickey and Minnie are wearing night shirts. They are marked "WALT DISNEY" and have their names on their chests.

PLATE 50
*Item A*: MICKEY MOUSE CHILD'S PURSE was made by the Cohn and Rosenberger Company. The purse is mesh with an enameled Mickey pin on the front. The rest of the coin purse is made of metal. *Item B*: MICKEY MOUSE BUBBLE BUSTER was manufactured by the Kilgore Company. This metal gun shop bubble buster bullets. The gun retailed for 25¢ and extra bubble sheets of 48 pops for 5¢. It is marked "WALT DISNEY ENTERPRISES."

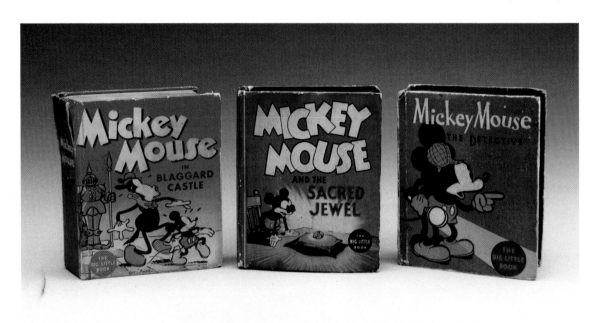

PLATE 51
MICKEY MOUSE LITTLE BIG BOOKS were published by The Whitman Company in the 1930's. They are all copyrighted Walt Disney Enterprises.

PLATE 52
PIN THE TAIL ON "MICKEY" GAME was played at parties. The object was to pin the tail on Mickey Mouse with each tail having a numerical value. It was made by The Marks Brothers Company of Boston.

PLATE 53
MICKEY MOUSE TREASURE CHEST BANK was made by The Crown Company. Mickey and the bank are made of composition. On the bottom is a metal latch that opened with a metal key to get the money out. It is marked "W.D. CROWN TOY."

PLATE 54
MICKEY MOUSE HOBBY CHIME PULL TOY was made by the N.N. Hill Brass Company. Mickey is made of wood; however, the rest of the toy is metal. It is marked in the middle of the wheel "c WALT DISNEY."

PLATE 55
WOODEN MICKEY MOUSE was made in Japan. Mickey's head is composition, his tail is string, his body is wood. His arms and legs are elastic and flexible. Mickey is 8" high. This piece is known by its four finger hands. It is marked "MICKEY MOUSE, WALT E DISNEY."

**PLATE 56**
MICKEY MOUSE THREE SECTIONAL DINNER PLATE was made by the Patriot China line of the Salem China Company. The plate is glazed and trimmed with a brown rim. Each section is marked "c WALT DISNEY".

PLATE 57
MICKEY MOUSE SCHOOL BLACKBOARD was manufactured by the Richmond School Furniture Company of Muncie, Indiana. The legs are made of wood. It is marked "c WALT DISNEY." It measures 20" high by 42".

PLATE 58
RUBBER MICKEY MOUSE AIRPLANE was made by the Sun Rubber Company. Mickey and the airplane are solid rubber. It is rare to find the propeller intact on this toy.

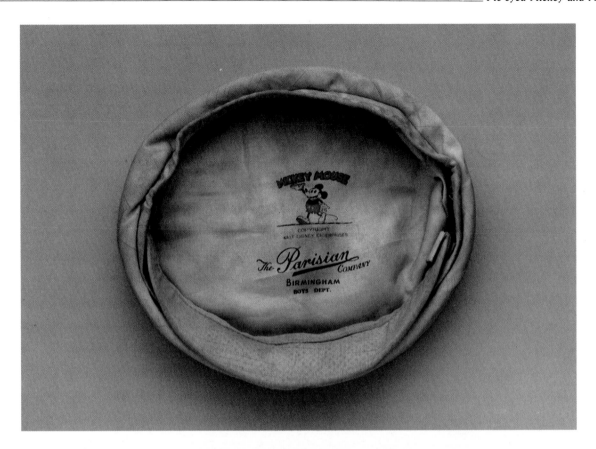

PLATE 59
MICKEY MOUSE CAP made for the Parisian Company, a Birmingham, Alabama, department store. It is marked "c
WALT DISNEY ENTERPRISES."

PLATE 60
MICKEY MOUSE CAP front view, described in Plate 59.

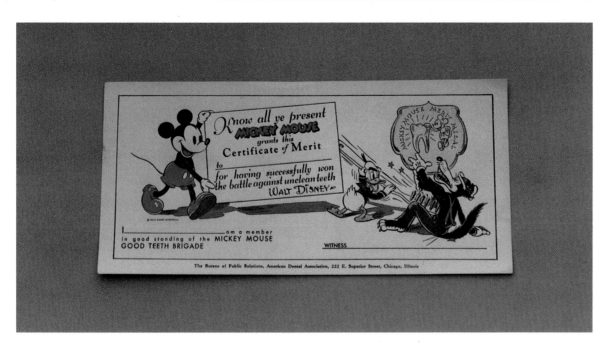

PLATE 61
MICKEY MOUSE DENTAL CERTIFICATE was given out by the American Dental Association in recognition of good dental hygiene. The child would then become a member of the Mickey Mouse Good Teeth Brigade. The certificate is marked "c WALT DISNEY ENTERPRISES."

PLATE 62
MICKEY MOUSE DOLL is made of felt and is European in orgin. Note the four finger gloved hands. There are no markings on this doll.

PLATE 63
MICKEY MOUSE AND MINNIE MOUSE
WOODEN FIGURES were made in Japan by
Fun-E-Flex. They all have wooden jointed
bodies, shoes, string tails and painted wooden
composition heads. The arms and legs are elastic
and flexible. The original flowers on Minnie are
extremely unusual as most were destroyed
through the years. They are all marked "WALT
E DISNEY."

PLATE 64
MICKEY MOUSE KNICKERBOCKER DOLL
was made by the Knickerbocker Toy Company.
The shoes are composition and the tail is wire.

PLATE 65
MICKEY MOUSE WOODEN CHRISTMAS ORNAMENT. The ears, arms and legs are elastic. There are no markings on this item.

PLATE 66
*Item A*: MICKEY MOUSE PENCIL BOX was made by the Dixon Company. This box is numbered "2909." It is marked "WALT DISNEY ENTERPRISES." *Item B*: MICKEY MOUSE PEN was made by The Inkograph Pen Company. The top of the pen is a composition Mickey head. The pen is marked "MICKEY MOUSE WALT E DISNEY."

PLATE 67
MICKEY MOUSE AND MINNIE MOUSE BISQUE FIGURES were made in Japan. They are hand painted and as a result, colors may vary on the same items.

# Long-billed Donald

After the incredible success of Mickey Mouse, the Disney studios were in dire need of some new characters to interact with Mickey. On June 9, 1934, Donald Duck made his film debut in The Wise Little Hen and since that memorable date, has become a mainstay in the Disney stable of characters. He has appeared in over 128 cartoons and 42 various other shorts.

Donald Duck became the ideal foil for Mickey's new found righteousness. His antics were so engaging and minus the discipline to which Mickey always had to adhere. Donald did those things that Mickey couldn't because it might tarnish Mickey's image. Donald Duck is Disney's most aggressive star. He is more like a duck in physical specifications and body than Mickey was a mouse or Goofy was a dog.

Disney himself summed up Donald Duck: "Donald's got a big mouth, big billigerent eyes, a twistable neck and a substantial backside that's highly flexible. The duck comes near being the animator's ideal subject. He's got plasticity plus."

This chapter depicts Donald Duck from 1934-1937.

Donald Duck from this period is identifiable by his long yellow bill and neck and his flat body. He is short and squatty with a waddling body. To indicate his mischievous nature one of his eyes was usually closed in a wink.

The super sensation that followed The Wise Little Hen propelled the same established merchandising machine that had mass produced Mickey and Minnie to start churning out Donald Duck toys and items. Donald quickly became Disney's second most famous character. Fewer Donald items were created during the vintage years because production didn't begin until 1934 compared to Mickey's start in 1928.

The most sought after Donald Duck merchandise is Donald with the long bill caught in his angry, devilish, boisterous poses.

The pictorial section of the Long-billed Donald chapter opens with a rare piece. Shown with its original box in *Plate 68* is waddling Donald Duck, an unusual celluloid tin wind up. When Donald is wound up, his body gyrates and he waddles forward. His head and body are made of celluloid and the tin wind up mechanism is encased in his body. This piece exemplifies early Donald Duck with his long bill, winking eye and duck like body. His hands are missing and in their place are wings. The original import sticker is on his tail marked "WADDLING DONALD DUCK, WALT DISNEY, JAPAN." As the box denotes, this toy was imported and distributed by the George Borgfeldt Corporation.

Another incredible celluloid tin wind up is pictured in *Plate 69*. Long-billed Donald being pulled by a celluloid Pluto is an excellent example of a tin toy adding a Disney character. In

this case, Donald and Pluto became an overnight sensation. When wound up, the toy moves forward at a rather fast pace. The whole cart is made of tin.

In *Plate 70* is the Lionel Donald Duck Handcar. This toy along with the Mickey and Minnie Handcar and the Mickey and Santa Handcar saved Lionel from bankruptcy. These trains reversed the down trend that conventional trains had taken. With the handcar came 72″ of track. It is marked "c WALT DISNEY." It is a collector's dream to have all three of the Lionel Handcars. In a recent auction, a record price of $2,800.00 was paid for this toy and its original box.

The Donald Duck toothbrush holder pictured in *Plate 71* is commonly referred to as "The Siamese Donald" toothbrush holder. It is made of bisque and is the only Disney toothbrush holder with a double image of the same character. "Siamese Donald" is hand painted and is marked "WALT DISNEY MADE IN JAPAN." There are two square holes; one in the back of each Donald Duck for toothbrushes.

A great example of a household item that generated sales by the use of a Disney character is the celluloid figural tape measure in *Plate 72*. The tape measure pulls out from Donald Duck's celluloid body. The tape iteself is marked "MADE IN JAPAN."

The Donald Duck pictured in *Plate 73* showed a different looking Donald in his standard sailor suit. It was manufactured by the Knickerbocker Toy Company. The doll is made of cloth with the hat, collar and bow tie made of felt. This particular Donald Duck doll has a look all its own and not seen in other Donald Duck toys of the 1930's.

PLATE 68
WADDLING DONALD DUCK CELLULOID WIND-UP was manufactured in Japan and distributed by the George Borgfeldt Corporation. Donald Duck is made of celluloid and the tin wind-up mechanism is encased in his body. It is marked "c WALT E DISNEY MADE IN JAPAN."

PLATE 69
LONG-BILLED DONALD AND PLUTO CELLULOID WIND-UP. This toy is extremely rare to find in good condition because celluloid was easily crushed by children playing with it. The cart is made of tin. The piece is marked "WALT DISNEY" on Donald's tail.

PLATE 70
DONALD DUCK HANDCAR was made by the Lionel Train Company. This is one of three handcars that saved The Lionel Company from bankruptcy. It is marked "WALT E DISNEY."

PLATE 71
DONALD DUCK BISQUE TOOTH-BRUSH HOLDER is known as the "Siamese Donald Toothbrush Holder." It was made in Japan and is marked "WALT E DISNEY."

PLATE 72
DONALD DUCK CELLULOID TAPE MEASURE is made entirely of celluloid. The tape measure pulls out of his body. It is marked "MADE IN JAPAN."

PLATE 73
DONALD DUCK KNICKERBOCKER CLOTH DOLL was made by The Knickerbocker Toy Company. It is 12″ tall and has a unique Donald Duck look. The doll is made of fabric except for the hat, collar and neck tie which are a felt-like material.

PLATE 74
DONALD DUCK LUSTERWARE ASHTRAY is made of a ceramic which has been glazed to give a very shiny effect. This piece was made in Japan and is marked "WALT E DISNEY." Occasionally, this piece will only have "MADE IN JAPAN" on the bottom but was still a licensed Disney piece.

PLATE 75
DONALD DUCK BISQUES are all hand painted and made in Japan. As pictured, they came in all sizes and varying poses and actions. Donald Duck on the scooter is harder to find than the other two.

PLATE 76
DONALD DUCK CARPET SWEEPER was manufactured by The Ohio Art Company. This child's toy is made of wood, and the lithography on the front of the sweeper is masterfully done. It is marked "c WALT DISNEY ENTERPRISES." The original bristles underneath actually allowed a child to simulate carpet sweeping.

PLATE 77
DONALD DUCK THREE SECTIONAL CHINA DINNER PLATE
was made by the Patriot Line of the Salem China Company.

PLATE 78
CELLULOID TIN WIND-UP DONALD DUCK. This toy is made
of celluloid with the feet being made of tin. When wound up,
Donald waddles forward. The key can be removed after winding.
The piece is marked "DONALD DUCK WALT DISNEY."

PLATE 79
DONALD DUCK SAND PAIL was made by The Ohio Art Company. It came with a matching sand shovel and was used when children went to the beach. The sand pail is made of tin and is marked "c 1938 W.D. Ent."

**PLATE 80**
MICKEY, MINNIE AND DONALD DUCK TOOTHBRUSH HOLDER is made of bisque. This is one of the few toothbrush holders that displays more than two Disney characters together. It is the only toothbrush holder displaying Mickey, Minnie and Donald.

PLATE 81
*Item A*: SQUEEZE TOY RUBBER DONALD DUCK was manufactured by The Seiberling Latex Rubber Company of Akron, Ohio. It is made of rubber but is hollow with a squeeze mechanism that when pushed, emits a sound. It is marked "c WALT DISNEY." *Item B*: SOLID RUBBER LONG-BILLED DONALD DUCK is also made by the Seiberling Latex Rubber Company. It is solid rubber and has a movable head. This piece is much heavier and also harder to find than the squeeze toy version.

PLATE 82
DONALD DUCK BIG LITTLE BOOK was published by the Whitman Publishing Company. There are many collectors who specialize in the acquisition of the various Big Little Books.

PLATE 83
DONALD DUCK BISQUE FIGURES were mass produced in Japan in the 1930's. Many of the Donald Duck bisques had his long bill stuck up in the air or his mouth in a talking position.

PLATE 84
DONALD DUCK MECHANICAL CHRISTMAS CARD was issued by the Whitman Publishing Company. During the 1930's these cards with envelopes sold for 5¢. On the front side of the card is a movable Donald that slides up and down; referred to as a mechanical card.

PLATE 85
DONALD DUCK SUN RUBBER TOYS were made by the Sun Rubber Company. They are solid rubber including the wheels. They are difficult to find with the heads intact. The hard rubber car is 6½″ long.

PLATE 86
DONALD DUCK CROWN SAVINGS BANK is made by The Crown Toy Company. Donald and the bank are made of composition. There is a metal latch that opened with a key on the bottom of the bank. Donald Duck's head is movable. It is marked "W.D. Crown Toy."

# Friends
# from the Golden Age

This chapter includes some of Pie-Eyed Mickey and Long-Billed Donald's good friends. All items are from the 1930's, the "Golden Age" of Disneyana collectibles, and are most sought after. There are many collectors who specialize and collect only Three Little Pigs or Snow White and The Seven Dwarfs memorabilia.

The Three Little Pigs came on to the scene during the hard hit days of the Depression in 1933. They were first seen in the cartoon film called "Three Little Pigs." The film was one of those made as a Silly Symphony and became the most famous one.

The American public could identify with the scared pigs and their continual search for security away from the big bad wolf. Many Americans felt the same pressure as times were hard and little money was available to pay the rent. R.D. Feild said of "Three Little Pigs" film: "No one will ever know to what extent the Three Little Pigs may be held responsible for pulling us out of the Depression; but certainly the lyrical jeer at the big bad wolf contributed not a little to the raising of people's spirits and to their defiance of circumstance!"

The public was so enthralled by the Three Little Pigs and the Big Bad Wolf that the same Disney merchandisers who had been mass producing Mickey and Donald set their machines into motion and they made many toys and novelties. The Three Little Pigs are best displayed in the toothbrush holder in Plate 101. There was Fifer who played his flute and built his house of straw; Fiddler who played the fiddle and built his house of sticks and Practical Pig who built his house of bricks and who sang the merry tune "Who's Afraid of the Big Bad Wolf" as he played a piano also made of bricks.

Pictured in *Plate 87* is one of the rarest pieces of The Three Little Pigs merchandise: the Who's Afraid of the Big Bad Wolf Alarm Clock. Along with the Mickey Mouse Alarm Clock, these were the first two produced by the Ingersoll-Waterbury Company in 1933. The success of these clocks and the Ingersoll watches saved the company from bankruptcy. The movement of the Big Bad Wolf's jaws, as it clicks open and shut with each tick of the clock, makes it a piece every collector wants on their shelf.

*Plate 95* is an excellent example of a boxed bisque set. To find bisques in their original boxes, enhances the value greatly. This is the largest set with each pig measuring 4½" tall. Pictured in *Plate 97* is an unusual Three Little Pigs ashtray and the brass match box holder. Disney quit production of anything related to cigarettes during the 1940's. The ashtray is made of ceramic that has been glazed and has the Disney copyright on the bottom.

Snow White was first released in 1937 and has been reissued constantly. It was the Disney studios first full length animated film. Walt Disney considered this film his masterpiece. The film debuted on December 21, 1937 and ran for five weeks at Radio City Music Hall. The first year Snow White earned 8.5 million dollars. The public adored the seven dwarfs: Doc, Grumpy, Sleepy, Bashful, Happy, Sneezy and Dopey. The most popular dwarf was Dopey and his items flooded the market.

By the time Snow White was released, the Depression was over, and the public had more money to spend. Snow White and the Seven Dwarfs were made into every imaginable product. Most pieces are marked "W D E", "WALT DISNEY ENTERPRISES" or "WALT DISNEY" but some of the latter 1939-1940 merchandise is marked "WDP."

Pictured in *Plate 88* is a Snow White and Seven Dwarfs boxed bisque set. This set is one of the smallest figurines produced with the Dwarfs being 2¾" and Snow White is 3½" tall. *Plate 90* is of a Dopey lamp created by the LaMode Studios of New York. The figural lamps of the 1930's are very rare and sought after. It is unusual to find one that has the original lamp shade attached. Pictured in *Plate 105* are Dopey and Happy ceramic bookends. These were made by the S. Maw, Son & Sons Company and produced in England. Disney items with foreign origin are very popular. The detail of this piece is exquisite.

Pinocchio was released on February 7, 1940, and the Disney Studio used new and unique procedures to animate this film. Pinocchio is known for its vibrant story line and memorable musical score. There was a massive amount of Pinocchio merchandise made in 1940, and it sold amazingly well. Pictured in *Plate 89* is a Knickerbocker composition Pinocchio. The original tag hangs from his hand. Composition has a tendency to crack through the years, but this piece is as mint as you will find.

PLATE 87
WHO'S AFRAID OF THE BIG BAD WOLF ALARM CLOCK was one of the first Disney clocks made by the Ingersoll-Waterbury Company. The wolf's animated jaws, click open and shut in rhythm with each tick of the clock. It is marked "Ingersoll MADE IN U.S.A."

PLATE 88
SNOW WHITE AND THE SEVEN DWARFS BISQUE SET. This boxed set is rare because of the sizes of the dwarfs and Snow White. The dwarfs are 2¾" tall and Snow White is 3½" tall. The box is marked "WALT DISNEY ENTERPRISES" and is extremely bright and colorful.

PLATE 89
KNICKERBOCKER COMPOSITION PINOCCHIO was made by the Knickerbocker Toy Company. Pinocchio is 10″ tall and is made of composition. The clothes are made of a combination of cloth and felt. The original tag hangs from his hand. Pinocchio is marked "WALT DISNEY'S PINOCCHIO c WDP 1938."

PLATE 90
DOPEY LAMP was manufactured by LaMode Studios of New York. It is made of modeware, a type of plaster. It is marked "WALT DISNEY ENTERPRISES" on a label on the bottom of the lamp and "c 1938 W.D.E." on the lamp base.

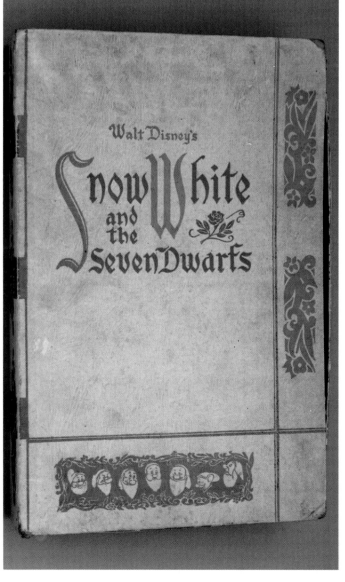

PLATE 91
SNOW WHITE AND THE SEVEN DWARFS FIGURAL SOAP was made
by The Lightfoot Schultz Company. Each figure is modeled in Castile Soap
and painted with harmless vegetable color.

PLATE 92
SNOW WHITE AND THE SEVEN DWARFS FIGURAL SOAP CON-
TAINER is made like a book. There is a gold leaf design on the front which
is made of a heavy cardboard. It opens up as if reading a book.

PLATE 93
SEIBERLING RUBBER PLUTOS are made by Seiberling Latex Rubber Company of Akron Ohio. To find one with a tail is very difficult. Pluto was produced in three sizes.

PLATE 94
THE SEVEN DWARF GLASSES are made by The Libbey Glass Company of Ohio. The images came in an array of colors and are marked "W.D."

PLATE 95
THE THREE LITTLE PIGS BOXED BISQUE SET was hand painted and made in Japan. The Three Little Pigs are 4½" tall and are each marked "c WALT DISNEY." They are each playing the musical instrument they are associated with.

PLATE 96
DOC, SNEEZY AND SLEEPY LARGE BISQUE FIGURES are each 5″ tall. They are marked "c WALT DISNEY." These are the largest size produced.

PLATE 97
*Item A*: THE THREE LITTLE PIGS LUSTER-WARE ASHTRAY is made of ceramic that has been glazed. It is marked on the bottom "c WALT DISNEY MADE IN JAPAN." *Item B*: THE THREE LITTLE PIGS MATCH BOX is made of brass and held on a small box of matches. It is marked on the back "c WALT DISNEY."

PLATE 98
DOPEY HAND PUPPET is made by The Crown Toy. His head is composition. It is marked "DOPEY WALT DISNEY ENT."

PLATE 99
LARGE PINOCCHIO BISQUE FIGURE is 5½″ tall. It is
marked "WALT DISNEY PROD" and was made in Japan.

PLATE 100
RUBBER SEVEN DWARFS were made by the Seiberling Latex Company. All are 5½″ tall and are made of
hard rubber. The Snow White of this set is hard to find
because she is hollow and of soft rubber and rarely held
up through the years.

PLATE 101
THREE LITTLE PIGS TOOTHBRUSH
HOLDER is made of bisque. The colors are
brighter than most bisques. It is marked "c
WALT DISNEY."

PLATE 102
SNOW WHITE AND THE SEVEN DWARFS
DRESS BUTTONS are made by the Hollywood
Company. The package is marked "W D ENT
1937."

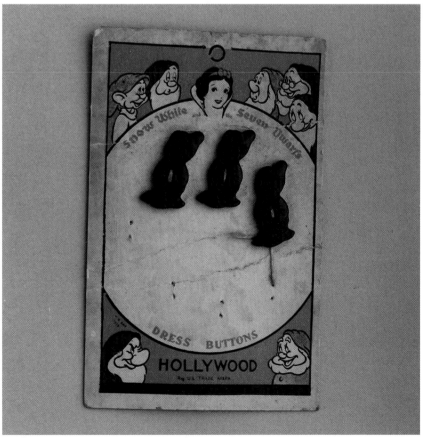

PLATE 103
SO WHO'S AFRAID OF THE BIG BAD WOLF BOOK BANK is made by The Zell Products Company of New York. The bank is made of metal and accepted both coins and bills. It is marked "WALT E DISNEY."

PLATE 104
FUN E FLEX WOODEN PLUTO is made in Japan and distributed by the George Borgfeldt Company. Pluto's ears are made of felt and his tail and legs of wire. It is marked on the decal "PLUTO THE PUP, WALT E DISNEY."

**PLATE 105**
DOPEY AND HAPPY BOOKENDS are made of a glazed ceramic by S. Maw, Son and Sons of England. They are very detailed and are marked on the bottom "GENUINE WALT DISNEY COPYRIGHT FOREIGN."

PLATE 106
SNOW WHITE AND THE SEVEN DWARFS
BISQUE SET. All the dwarfs in this set are 3½″
tall and Snow White is 4½″ tall. Each figure
has their name on the front of the hat. The backs
are all marked "WALT DISNEY"

PLATE 107
CHALK PLUTO FIGURE was made and hand
painted in Japan. It is marked "c WALT
DISNEY."

PLATE 108
THREE LITTLE PIGS TOOTHBRUSH
HOLDERS highlight Practical Pig, Fiddler Pig
and Fifer Pig in bisque. The holes for the
toothbrushes are in the back of the holder.

PLATE 109
THE THREE LITTLE PIGS BRIDGE SCORE
SHEET was made by the Western P&L Com-
pany of Racine, Wisconsin in 1932. It is mark-
ed on the front "c FROM THREE LITTLE PIGS
THE WALT DISNEY SILLY SYMPHONY."

PLATE 110
THE THREE LITTLE PIGS CHINA SECTIONAL
DINNER PLATE is made by the Patriot Division of
the Salem China Company. The plate has a blue rim
around it. Each section is marked "WALT DISNEY"
in script.

PLATE 111
PLUTO AND MICKEY MOUSE TOOTHBRUSH
HOLDER was made in Japan. There is a trough
where the toothbrush could be placed. It is marked
"c WALT E DISNEY" on the back.

# Later Merchandise

The final chapter of this book deals with Disney merchandise and memorabilia from 1940 to 1987. Earlier merchandise from this period is becoming highly collectible and the prices are increasing almost daily. Most memorabilia from this period is affordable. Beware of 1960 and 1970 items. Many dealers are charging prices that exceed what they charge currently for the same items at the theme parks.

The nostalgia market for the 1950's items is growing at a quick rate. Many collectors seek merchandise from feature films of this era—Davy Crockett, 1955; Lady and the Tramp, 1955 and Sleeping Beauty, 1959.

Most of the best 1950's merchandise is from the Mickey Mouse Club that was on television daily from 5:00 to 6:00 p.m. The show started on October 3, 1955. Mickey Mouse went from a movie star to a television star overnight. Mickey Mouse Club merchandise abounded in every imaginable item.

There are instant collectibles from the 1960's and 1970's. These are pieces that are produced on a limited run and are more valuable immediately. For example, the Schmid Company produces new sets yearly on a limited run. Many specialty items have been created for Mickey Mouse and Donald Duck's 50th birthdays. Collectors seek the different pins and buttons produced for special events at the theme parks.

All items produced after September 29, 1938 are marked "WALT DISNEY PRODUCTIONS" or "W.D.P." No one dealer will price items after this date the same way. There were literally thousands of items produced during this era. A boxed item will appreciate much quicker than one without.

In this chapter, I have tried to picture a cross sampling

of various merchandise of each decade after the "golden decade" of the 1930's. I have also attempted to give a cross sampling of the differentials in price based on the rareness and collectibility of the item.

Pictured in *Plate 115* is Donald Duck Drummer, a tin wind up, manufactured by the Line Mar Company. Disney tin wind ups command a huge price as they are sought by Disney collectors and tin wind up collectors. They are not easy to find in good and working condition. In *Plate 119* are a Mickey and Minnie Mouse figurine made by the American Pottery Company. Ceramics made by this company, Evan K. Shaw, Brayton's Laguna Pottery, Leeds China Company, Hagen Renaker and Vernon Kilns are very popular and not easily found. Pottery figures are a collectible field unto itself.

In *Plate 121* is pictured a Mickey Mouse Goebel figurine. The Goebel Company, most famous for their Hummel figurines, produced a number of Disney pieces; always in limited numbers. The markings date this piece and do much in determining its value. In *Plate 138* is a Donald Duck Crown Staffordshire limited edition plate commemorating Donald's 50th birthday. These limited edition items become instant collectibles and their value immediately increases.

Pictured in *Plate 148* is a Donald Duck movie cel. Collecting movie celluloids is a different facet of Disneyana. Early cels can go for up to $30,000.00. It is a very specialized field. Many large auction companies hold yearly cel auctions and each year the prices realized set new records.

In *Plate 160* is a Mickey Mouse Schmid music box that was also a limited edition article.

PLATE 112
MICKEY MOUSE AND DONALD DUCK BENDY DOLLS are made of foam rubber and produced in England. All parts of the body are flexible.

PLATE 113
DONALD DUCK BANK was made in 1979 by Play Pal Plastics. There is a slot in Donald's hat to deposit coins.

PLATE 114
YOUR TRIP TO DISNEYLAND ON RECORDS was made by The Mattel Toy Company. The set included five records plus a giant full-color panorama of Disneyland.

PLATE 115
DONALD DUCK DRUMMER is a tin wind-up, manufactured by Line Mar Company. Disney tin wind-ups are sought after by many toy collectors.

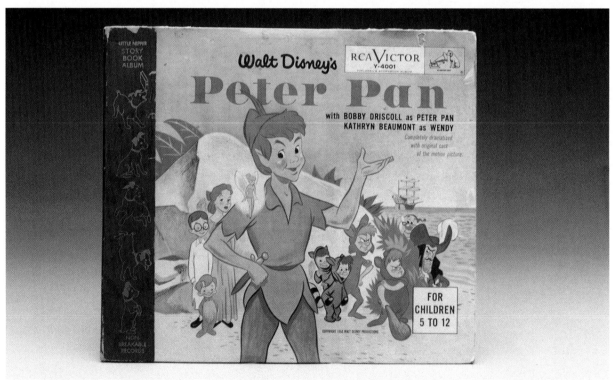

PLATE 116
DISNEY CHARACTER PUPPETS were manufactured by the Gund Manufacturing Company. The heads are made of hard plastic, and the outfits are made of cloth. The puppets are each marked "WDP" on their necks.

PLATE 117
PETER PAN STORY BOOK ALBUM was recorded in 1952 by RCA Victor. It was from the Little Nipper series which included a record album and storybook with graphic color pages. This was the original cast recording.

PLATE 118
MICKEY MOUSE CHOO CHOO was made by The Fisher Price Company. It is number 485. The wooden wheels indicate the toy was made in the 1940's-1950's.

PLATE 119
MICKEY AND MINNIE MOUSE ceramic figurines were made by the American Pottery Company. They are marked "WALT DISNEY PRO-DUCTIONS" and are very collectible.

**PLATE 120**
MICKEY AND MINNIE MOUSE ACROBATS were made in Occupied Japan. The figures are made of celluloid. Mickey and Minnie are marked "OCCUPIED JAPAN" on their necks. This is a very rare and unusual latter day toy.

PLATE 121
MICKEY MOUSE GOEBEL FIGURINE was made by the Goebel Company, the German company famous for Hummel figurines. This piece is marked with a "FULLBEE" mark (a bee in the letter V) on the underside along with the word "GERMANY."

PLATE 122
MICKEY MOUSE MARIONETTE was manufactured by Peter Puppet Playthings, Inc. of New York. Mickey is made of wood. The original box is very colorful.

PLATE 123
*Item A*: DONALD DUCK ROLY POLY is made of hard plastic. It has a round weighted bottom to keep it upright when a baby attempts to knock it over. *Item B*: DONALD DUCK SAVINGS BANK is made of plastic. There is a slot in the back to deposit coins.

PLATE 124
MICKEY MOUSE WALL CLOCK was made by the Elgin Company. The rim is made of hard plastic. It runs by electricity.

PLATE 125
MICKEY MOUSE KALEIDOSCOPE was made in the 1950's. Each turn creates a different design highlighted by small Mickey Mouses. The outside graphics are crisp and bright.

PLATE 126
LUDWIG VON DRAKE AND DONALD DUCK FIGURES were made by The Marx Company. The hands, arms, head and legs are flexible and bendable.

PLATE 127
SLEEPING BEAUTY MASQUERADE COSTUME was made by Ben Cooper, Inc., who made various Disney character costumes. The mask is plastic, and the costume is colorful cloth.

PLATE 128
MICKEY MOUSE POCKET WATCH was
made in Great Britain which makes this piece
more valuable than a comparable one made
in the U.S.A.

PLATE 129
MICKEY AND MINNIE MOUSE TALKING
DOLLS were made by the Knickerbocker
Toy Company. The Mickey Mouse Club
emblem is on their chests. To make Mickey
or Minnie talk, a pull string is located on
their backs.

PLATE 130
GOOFY AND MICKEY MOUSE
NODDERS were made by the Marx
Company. Both heads nod when
figures are moved.

PLATE 131
DONALD DUCK T.V. SAVINGS
BANK was made as an original by the
Dan Brechner Company. It is made of
ceramic that has been glazed.

PLATE 132
MICKEY MOUSE NAUTILUS SOAP BRUSH is unmarked. The ship is made of rubber and the bottom is a soap brush to be used in the bathtub.

PLATE 133
DISNEY LITTLE GOLDEN BOOKS were published starting in 1942. There are many cover and internal revisions of the more popular titles. Some original books of 42 pages were slimmed down to 28 pages.

PLATE 134
DONALD DUCK CHOO CHOO was made by
The Fisher Price Company. It is numbered
"No 450." As the cart moves, the hammer hits
the bell.

PLATE 135
MICKEY MOUSE CLOTH DOLL was made
by the Stacee-Lee Company of Brooklyn, New
York. It was made of cellulose fiber and syn-
thetic foam.

PLATE 136
MICKEY MOUSE WRIST WATCH was made by the Ingersoll Watch Company/Timex from 1968 to 1971. Any watch made by Ingersoll is highly collectable.

PLATE 137
MICKEY MOUSE CAMERA AND MICK-O-MATIC CAMERA both use 35mm film and are great cameras for kids to use.

PLATE 138
DONALD DUCK PLATE made by the Crown Staffordshire Company of England to commemorate Donald's 50th birthday. It is made of fine bone china.

PLATE 139
WALT DISNEY CARTOON THEATRE was made by Sawyers and used View Master films. The back of the box served as a screen for the projector.

PLATE 140
MICKEY MOUSE CLUB CAR was made by the Knicker-
bocker Toy Company in 1976. The car is made of cloth.
The horn is a rubber Pluto that squeaks when pressed.

PLATE 141
DONALD DUCK GUNSLINGER was made by Mavco Toy
Company. Donald is made of plastic and the wind-up
mechanism is encased in Donald's rear.

PLATE 142
*Item A*: GOOFY SAVINGS BANK was made by Plastic Play Pals Company. It is made of hard rubber. *Item B*: DONALD DUCK BANK was made in Japan and is made of glazed ceramic.

PLATE 143
DOLLY TOY PIN UPS were manufactured by the Dolly Toy Company. The pin ups were commonly used on nursery walls.

PLATE 144
DAVY CROCKETT IRON ON EMBLEMS
DISPLAY CARD. These patches were used
by parents for kids on clothing. They could
be put on by using a hot iron.

PLATE 145
MICKEY MOUSE ALARM CLOCK was
made by the Ingersoll Watch Company. The
base is metal and also came in green and red.

PLATE 146
MICKEY MOUSE AND DONALD DUCK PLASTIC FIGURES are very common. They were mass produced in the 1960's and 1970's. Most were made in Japan, Korea and Taiwan.

PLATE 147
*Item A*: MICKEY MOUSE MINIATURE CAR was made by the Marx Company. *Item B*: ROLYKINS were made by Louis Marx and Company. The bottoms are weighed with ball bearing action. When hit, they will bounce back. *Item C*: DONALD DUCK MATCHBOX TOY was made by The Matchbox Toy Company. There is a complete set of different matchbox Disney characters.

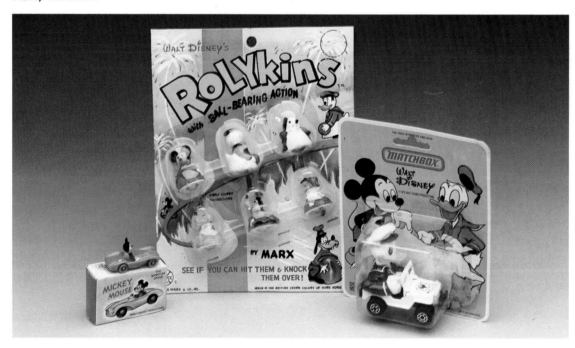

PLATE 148
DONALD DUCK MOVIE CEL is an original hand painted celluloid drawing actually used in a Walt Disney production. It is marked "YOURS FOR PARTICIPATING IN INA SEPT 1 - NOV 30, 1959, DISNEYLAND."

PLATE 149
MICKEY MOUSE MAGIC DIVIDER game was made by Jaymar Company and tied in as an educational toy with the Mickey Mouse Club. The problems are solved by electricity.

PLATE 150
MICKEY MOUSE XYLOPHONE is a wind-up made by Marx Company. Mickey is plastic and the rest of the piece is tin. The all metal version is more valuable.

PLATE 151
DONALD DUCK TALKING TOY was made by Hassenfeld Brothers, Inc. Donald says eight different phrases when his string is pulled. His eyes and arms change positions when Donald talks.

**PLATE 152**
MICKEY MOUSE CLUB MEMORABILIA. All of these items were made for the 1970's version of the Mickey Mouse Club. They are very common and should be priced and bought accordingly.

**PLATE 153**
*Item A*: GOOFY CHRISTMAS LIGHT is made of plastic and is illuminated when plugged in. *Item B*: PINOCCHIO SOAKY was made by the Colgate Palmolive Company and contained bubble bath. Soakys were produced displaying many different Disney characters.

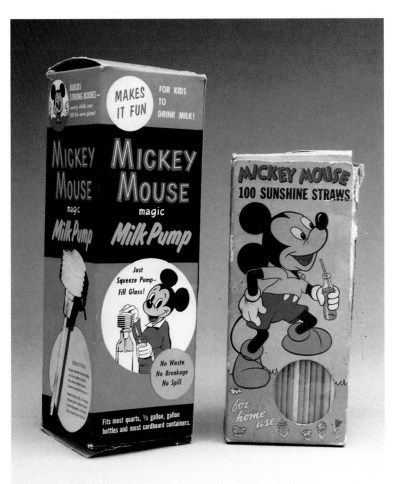

PLATE 154
*Item A*: MICKEY MOUSE MILK PUMP was used by children to prevent milk bottle breakage and spills. It also promoted the drinking of milk. It was made by the Morris Plastic Company. *Item B*: MICKEY MOUSE SUNSHINE STRAWS were made by The Herz Manufacturing Corporation in the 1950's. One hundred straws cost 10¢.

PLATE 155
MICKEY MOUSE CLUB DRUM AND TAMBOURINE were manufactured by the Noble & Cooley Company. They were used by kids as they watched the Mickey Mouse Club.

PLATE 156
*Item A*: DONALD DUCK CAR was made by the Kohner Company in 1973. The vehicle is hard plastic. Donald is made of hard rubber. *Item B*: MICKEY MOUSE POP UP PIANO was manufactured by the Gabriel Toy Company.

PLATE 157
DONALD DUCK SKEDIDDLER was made by the Mattel Toy Company. When pushed, Donald's arms, legs and head move.

PLATE 158
SNOW WHITE AND SCHOOL BUS LUNCH
BOXES were made by the Aladdin Company.
A lunch box's value is enchanced by having the
thermos.

PLATE 159
MICKEY MOUSE WATER BALL was made by
The Jolly Blinker Company and was used as a
bathtub toy. It floats on top of the water.

PLATE 160
MICKEY MOUSE MUSIC BOX was made by the
Schmid Company. Schmid manufactures limited
runs on Disney items. This is No. 203 of the
musical collection series. It plays the Mickey
Mouse Club theme song.

PLATE 161
MICKEY MOUSE ALARM CLOCKS are both
made by the Bradley Company in West Germany.

PLATE 162
POP-UP PLUTO was made by The Fisher Price Company. Pluto moves when the string is pulled.

# Price Guide
# &
# Supplemental Price Guide

# Price Guide

The price guide for Disneyana collectibles is to be used as a point of reference before buying or selling an item. Any price guide tends to be subjective in nature, and I've used the sources available to me to arrive at what I think are accurate price points in today's marketplace. This Disney toy market can change dramatically in a very short span of time.

I have determined the prices for each item based on a number of factors and sources:

1. What I paid for each item.
2. Auction catalogs.
3. Mail auction price realized lists.
4. Toy and doll show prices.
5. Antique trader ads.

I feel the prices suggested are excellent estimations of what each item is actually worth. The basic law of economics, supply and demand, can shoot holes through any price guide. The adage that the worth of a toy is what someone will pay for it is still prevalent for today's collectors. Emotion and the strong desire of wanting to add a certain piece to your collection will result in paying more. The following descriptions relate to the condition of the toy and how they are priced accordingly.

## GOOD CONDITION

The toy is in working order, has been used, shows general wear and tear. The toy must look fairly clean with little or no rust.

## EXCELLENT, MINT CONDITION

The toy is clean and looks as if it was never used. It is complete and all functions are operative. Mint applies to mint in the box (MIB) and means the toy is in its original packaging. In many cases, the box is worth more than the item itself.

| Photo | Item | Good | Excellent/ Mint |
|---|---|---|---|
| Plate 1 | Rambling Mickey Mouse | $7,500.00 | $10,000.00 |
| Plate 2 | Mickey & Minnie Acrobats | 1,000.00 | 1,200.00 |
| Plate 3 | Lionel Mickey & Minnie Handcar | 1,200.00 | 1,500.00 |
| Plate 4 | Mickey Mouse Wrist Watch | 800.00 | 1,000.00 |
| Plate 5 | Mickey Mouse Wrist Watch | 800.00 | 1,000.00 |
| Plate 6 | Mickey Mouse 9½" Bisque | 4,500.00 | 5,000.00 |
| Plate 7 | Mickey Mouse Bisque Toothbrush Holder | 300.00 | 450.00 |
| Plate 8 | Mickey Mouse Bisque Toothbrush Holder | 300.00 | 450.00 |
| Plate 9 | Minnie Mouse Bisque Toothbrush Holder | 275.00 | 400.00 |
| Plate 10 | Minnie Mouse Bisque Toothbrush Holder | 275.00 | 400.00 |
| Plate 11 | Mickey Mouse Post Office Bank | 100.00 | 150.00 |
| Plate 12 | The Three Pals Bisque Set In Box | 700.00 | 1,200.00 |
| Plate 13 | Mickey Mouse Tea Set (Complete) | 400.00 | 450.00 |
| Plate 14 | Mickey Mouse Tea Set (Complete) | 400.00 | 450.00 |
| Plate 15 | Wood and Composition Mickey Mouse | 900.00 | 1,200.00 |
| Plate 16 | Mickey Mouse Child's Potty | 350.00 | 450.00 |
| Plate 17 | Rocking Horse Mickey Mouse | 3,000.00 | 3,500.00 |
| Plate 18 | Mickey Mouse Jam Jar Bank | 75.00 | 100.00 |
| Plate 19 | Mickey Mouse Hand Puppet | 1,500.00 | 2,000.00 |
| Plate 20 | Mickey Mouse Telephone | 110.00 | 150.00 |
| Plate 21 | Mickey Mouse Dollhouse | 125.00 | 165.00 |
| Plate 22 | Mickey Mouse Musician Bisque | 60.00 | 85.00 |
| Plate 23 | Mickey Mouse & Minnie Mouse Glass Tumblers | 100.00 | 110.00 |
| Plate 24 | Mickey Mouse Dominoes | 75.00 | 100.00 |
| Plate 25 | Mickey Mouse Lusterware Ashtray | 175.00 | 225.00 |
| Plate 26 | Mickey & Minnie Mouse Toothbrush Holder | 200.00 | 230.00 |
| Plate 27 | Item A – Large Rubber Mickey Mouse | 175.00 | 200.00 |
| | Item B – Small Rubber Mickey Mouse | 110.00 | 120.00 |
| Plate 28 | Mickey Mouse Target | 65.00 | 80.00 |
| Plate 29 | Minnie Mouse Celluloid Doll | 300.00 | 350.00 |
| Plate 30 | Mickey Mouse Transfer-O-S | 35.00 | 50.00 |
| Plate 31 | Mickey Mouse Print Shop | 75.00 | 100.00 |
| Plate 32 | Mickey Mouse Needlecraft | 55.00 | 65.00 |
| Plate 33 | Minnie Mouse China Mug | 45.00 | 60.00 |
| Plate 34 | Mickey Mouse Figural Soap | 95.00 | 120.00 |
| Plate 35 | Item A – Mickey Mouse Sand Pail | 100.00 | 110.00 |
| | Item B – Mickey Mouse Beach Bag | 70.00 | 75.00 |
| Plate 36 | Mickey Mouse Hoop-La Game | 200.00 | 225.00 |
| Plate 37 | Mickey Mouse Pop-Up Book | 150.00 | 175.00 |
| Plate 38 | Pop-Up Scene | 25.00 | 50.00 |
| Plate 39 | Mickey Mouse Knickerbocker Doll | 400.00 | 450.00 |
| Plate 40 | Mickey Mouse Drum | 150.00 | 175.00 |
| Plate 41 | Mickey Mouse Look-A-Like | 25.00 | 35.00 |
| Plate 42 | Mickey, Minnie & Pluto Toothbrush Holder | 175.00 | 225.00 |
| Plate 43 | Item A – Mickey Mouse Hair Brush | 40.00 | 50.00 |

| | | | |
|---|---|---|---|
| | Item B – Mickey Mouse Bar Soap ..............................45.00 | | 55.00 |
| Plate 44 | Mickey Mouse Silver Spoon ......25.00 | | 30.00 |
| Plate 45 | Item A – Mickey Mouse Baby Rattle ............................200.00 | | 250.00 |
| | Item B – Mickey Mouse Baby Rattle ............................300.00 | | 325.00 |
| Plate 46 | Mickey & Minnie Carpet Sweeper ............................95.00 | | 120.00 |
| Plate 47 | Wooden 6½" Mickey Mouse ....200.00 | | 225.00 |
| Plate 48 | Mickey Mouse Film ..................25.00 | | 35.00 |
| Plate 49 | Mickey & Minnie Bisques (Pair) ..............................110.00 | | 130.00 |
| Plate 50 | Item A – Mickey Mouse Child's Purse .........................225.00 | | 250.00 |
| | Item B – Mickey Mouse Bubble Buster ......................200.00 | | 225.00 |
| Plate 51 | Mickey Mouse Little Big Books ........................35.00 | | 60.00 |
| Plate 52 | Pin The Tail on Mickey ............50.00 | | 60.00 |
| Plate 53 | Mickey Mouse Crown Bank ....260.00 | | 275.00 |
| Plate 54 | Mickey Mouse Pull Toy ..........300.00 | | 350.00 |
| Plate 55 | Wooden Mickey Mouse 8" .......650.00 | | 750.00 |
| Plate 56 | Mickey Mouse Dinner Plate ....100.00 | | 115.00 |
| Plate 57 | Mickey Mouse Blackboard ......300.00 | | 320.00 |
| Plate 58 | Rubber Mickey Mouse Airplane ..............................65.00 | | 85.00 |
| Plate 59 | Mickey Mouse Cap ..................160.00 | | 170.00 |
| Plate 60 | Mickey Mouse Cap ..................160.00 | | 170.00 |
| Plate 61 | Mickey Mouse Dental Certificate ......................15.00 | | 20.00 |
| Plate 62 | Mickey Mouse Doll ..................110.00 | | 130.00 |
| Plate 63 | Mickey Mouse Wooden Figure ..............................125.00 | | 150.00 |
| Plate 64 | Mickey Mouse Knickerbocker Doll ................400.00 | | 550.00 |
| Plate 65 | Mickey Mouse Christmas Ornament ..........................85.00 | | 95.00 |
| Plate 66 | Item A – Mickey Mouse Pencil Box ..............................125.00 | | 135.00 |
| | Item B – Mickey Mouse Pen ...100.00 | | 110.00 |
| Plate 67 | Mickey Mouse Bisque Figure ....50.00 | | 65.00 |
| Plate 68 | Waddling Donald Duck ........3,600.00 | | 4,000.00 |
| Plate 69 | Donald & Pluto Tin Wind-Up ..................1,200.00 | | 1,500.00 |
| Plate 70 | Donald Duck Lionel Handcar ..................1,500.00 | | 1,800.00 |
| Plate 71 | Donald Duck Bisque Toothbrush Holder ................300.00 | | 325.00 |
| Plate 72 | Donald Duck Tape Measure ....250.00 | | 275.00 |
| Plate 73 | Donald Duck Knickerbocker Doll ................260.00 | | 280.00 |
| Plate 74 | Donald Duck Ashtray .............210.00 | | 220.00 |
| Plate 75 | Donald Duck Bisques (each) .....55.00 | | 80.00 |
| Plate 76 | Donald Duck Carpet Sweeper ..............................95.00 | | 110.00 |
| Plate 77 | Donald Duck Dinner Plate ......110.00 | | 125.00 |
| Plate 78 | Celluloid Tin Donald Duck Wind Up ..............................400.00 | | 450.00 |
| Plate 79 | Donald Duck Sand Pail ............80.00 | | 90.00 |
| Plate 80 | Mickey, Minnie & Donald Toothbrush Holder .................275.00 | | 310.00 |
| Plate 81 | Item A – Rubber Donald Duck Squeeze Toy ..................200.00 | | 225.00 |
| | Item B – Rubber Donald Duck ...........................250.00 | | 275.00 |
| Plate 82 | Donald Duck Little Big Book ....40.00 | | 55.00 |
| Plate 83 | Donald Duck Bisques ...............55.00 | | 80.00 |
| Plate 84 | Donald Duck Christmas Card ...25.00 | | 30.00 |
| Plate 85 | Donald Duck Sun Rubber Toy ......................45.00 | | 65.00 |
| Plate 86 | Donald Duck Crown Bank ......260.00 | | 275.00 |
| Plate 87 | Who's Afraid of the Big Bad Wolf Alarm Clock ....................900.00 | | 950.00 |
| Plate 88 | Snow White & The Seven Dwarfs Bisque Set ...................275.00 | | 350.00 |
| Plate 89 | Knickerbocker Composition Pinocchio ................................400.00 | | 425.00 |
| Plate 90 | Dopey LaMode Lamp .............125.00 | | 140.00 |
| Plate 91 | Snow White Figural Soap .......200.00 | | 225.00 |
| Plate 92 | Snow White Figural Soap Box ....................100.00 | | 115.00 |
| Plate 93 | Seiberling Rubber Plutos ..........50.00 | | 75.00 |
| Plate 94 | The Seven Dwarf Glasses (each) ......................25.00 | | 30.00 |
| Plate 95 | The Three Little Pigs Boxed Bisque Set ...................350.00 | | 400.00 |
| Plate 96 | Large Dwarf Bisques ...............50.00 | | 65.00 |
| Plate 97 | Item A – The Three Little Pigs Ashtray ...........................90.00 | | 110.00 |
| | Item B – The Three Little Pigs Match Box ..........................75.00 | | 85.00 |
| Plate 98 | Dopey Hand Puppet ..................50.00 | | 60.00 |
| Plate 99 | Pinocchio Bisque Figure ..........70.00 | | 85.00 |
| Plate 100 | Rubber Dwarfs (each) ...............35.00 | | 45.00 |
| Plate 101 | The Three Little Pigs Toothbrush Holder .................150.00 | | 170.00 |
| Plate 102 | Snow White and The Seven Dwarfs Press Buttons ...............45.00 | | 55.00 |
| Plate 103 | Who's Afraid of The Big Bad Wolf Bank ..........................95.00 | | 100.00 |
| Plate 104 | Fun E Flex Wooden Pluto .......220.00 | | 230.00 |
| Plate 105 | Dopey & Happy Bookends ......210.00 | | 220.00 |
| Plate 106 | Snow White & The Seven Dwarfs Bisque Set ...................400.00 | | 475.00 |
| Plate 107 | Chalk Pluto .............................20.00 | | 25.00 |
| Plate 108 | Three Little Pigs Toothbrush Holder .................110.00 | | 125.00 |
| Plate 109 | Three Little Pigs Bridge Score Sheet ..........................45.00 | | 55.00 |
| Plate 110 | Three Little Pigs Dinner Plate ...85.00 | | 95.00 |
| Plate 111 | Pluto & Mickey Toothbrush Holder ..............................225.00 | | 250.00 |
| Plate 112 | Mickey or Donald Bendy Doll ..............................60.00 | | 70.00 |
| Plate 113 | Donald Duck Bank ..................15.00 | | 20.00 |
| Plate 114 | Your Trip to Disneyland On Records ............................25.00 | | 30.00 |

| Plate 115 | Donald Duck Drummer | 375.00 | 450.00 |
|---|---|---|---|
| Plate 116 | Disney Character Puppets | 10.00 | 15.00 |
| Plate 117 | Peter Pan Storybook Album | 25.00 | 30.00 |
| Plate 118 | Mickey Mouse Choo Choo | 40.00 | 50.00 |
| Plate 119 | Mickey & Minnie Ceramic Figures | 120.00 | 135.00 |
| Plate 120 | Mickey & Minnie Acrobats | 600.00 | 750.00 |
| Plate 121 | Mickey Mouse Figurine, Goebel | 275.00 | 300.00 |
| Plate 122 | Mickey Mouse Marionette | 75.00 | 100.00 |
| Plate 123 | Item A – Donald Duck Roly Poly | 5.00 | 10.00 |
| | Item B – Donald Duck Savings Bank | 5.00 | 10.00 |
| Plate 124 | Mickey Mouse Wall Clock | 15.00 | 20.00 |
| Plate 125 | Mickey Mouse Kaleidoscope | 34.00 | 45.00 |
| Plate 126 | Uncle Scrooge & Donald Plastic Figures | 20.00 | 25.00 |
| Plate 127 | Sleeping Beauty Costume | 15.00 | 20.00 |
| Plate 128 | Mickey Mouse Pocket Watch | 40.00 | 50.00 |
| Plate 129 | Mickey & Minnie Knickerbocker Dolls | 30.00 | 35.00 |
| Plate 130 | Goofy & Mickey Nodders, Marx | 30.00 | 40.00 |
| Plate 131 | Donald Duck TV Savings Bank | 35.00 | 40.00 |
| Plate 132 | Mickey Mouse Nautilus Soap Brush | 15.00 | 20.00 |
| Plate 133 | Little Golden Books | 5.00 | 10.00 |
| Plate 134 | Donald Duck Choo Choo | 40.00 | 50.00 |
| Plate 135 | Mickey Mouse Cloth Doll | 5.00 | 10.00 |
| Plate 136 | Mickey Mouse Wrist Watch | 200.00 | 225.00 |
| Plate 137 | Mickey Mouse Camera | 30.00 | 35.00 |
| Plate 138 | Donald Duck Plate | 20.00 | 25.00 |
| Plate 139 | Cartoon Theater | 35.00 | 40.00 |
| Plate 140 | Mickey Mouse Club Car | 25.00 | 30.00 |
| Plate 141 | Donald Duck Gunslinger | 125.00 | 150.00 |
| Plate 142 | Item A – Goofy Savings Bank | 10.00 | 15.00 |
| | Item B – Donald Duck Bank | 5.00 | 10.00 |
| Plate 143 | Dolly Toy Pin Ups | 30.00 | 35.00 |
| Plate 144 | Davy Crockett Iron On | 15.00 | 20.00 |
| Plate 145 | Mickey Mouse Alarm Clock | 200.00 | 225.00 |
| Plate 146 | Mickey & Donald Plastic Figures | 5.00 | 10.00 |
| Plate 147 | Item A – Mickey Mouse Miniature Car | 10.00 | 12.00 |
| | Item B – Rolykins | 25.00 | 30.00 |
| | Item C – Match Box Toy | 10.00 | 15.00 |
| Plate 148 | Donald Duck Movie Cel | 150.00 | 175.00 |
| Plate 149 | Mickey Mouse Magic Divider | 10.00 | 15.00 |
| Plate 150 | Mickey Mouse Xylophone | 475.00 | 550.00 |
| Plate 151 | Donald Duck Talking Toy | 15.00 | 20.00 |
| Plate 152 | Mickey Mouse Club Memorabilia | 3.00 | 10.00 |
| Plate 153 | Item A – Goofy Christmas Light | 10.00 | 15.00 |
| | Item B – Pinocchio Soaky | 5.00 | 10.00 |
| Plate 154 | Item A – Mickey Mouse Milk Pump | 15.00 | 20.00 |
| | Item B – Mickey Mouse Straws | 5.00 | 10.00 |
| Plate 155 | Mickey Mouse Club Drum & Tamborine | 15.00 | 20.00 |
| Plate 156 | Item A – Donald Duck Car | 5.00 | 10.00 |
| | Item B – Mickey Mouse Pop Up Piano | 5.00 | 10.00 |
| Plate 157 | Donald Duck Skediddler | 15.00 | 20.00 |
| Plate 158 | Disney Lunch Boxes | 15.00 | 20.00 |
| Plate 159 | Mickey Mouse Water Ball | 20.00 | 25.00 |
| Plate 160 | Mickey Mouse Music Box | 200.00 | 225.00 |
| Plate 161 | Bradley Alarm Clocks | 35.00 | 40.00 |
| Plate 162 | Pop Up Pluto | 15.00 | 20.00 |

# Supplemental Price Guide

### Pie-Eyed Mickey Mouse

Bagatelle, marbles, super graphics Marks Bros ............ $150.00-175.00

Balls, Seiberling Latex Rubber Co ....................................... 30.00-35.00

Banks, treasure chest. brown fabric covering

    Zell Products ............................................................ 140.00-150.00

    Dime register, tin lithograph ................................... 250.00-275.00

    Cast iron, 9½" ................................................... 1,950.00-2,000.00

Belts, heavy metal buckle, Hickok Mfg. Co .................. 60.00-65.00

Biscuit Tin, Australian, metal lithograph ..................... 150.00-200.00

Bisque, porcelain, made in Japan and distributed

by Geo. Borgfeldt Company

    Mickey Mouse (1–1¼") waving right hand ................. 75.00-100.00

    Mickey Mouse riding in canoe .............................. 2,000.00-2,500.00

    Mickey Mouse sitting ................................................ 160.00-165.00

    Mickey Mouse holding rifle ...................................... 160.00-165.00

    Mickey Mouse with baseball bat ................................. 200.00-225.00

    Mickey Mouse with catcher's mitt .............................. 200.00-225.00

    Mickey Mouse (3¼") holding musical instrument ........ 100.00-110.00

    Mickey Mouse with top hat and cane ........................... 70.00-90.00

    Mickey Mouse (4") in tuxedo with cane ....................... 70.00-90.00

    Mickey Mouse standing next to garbage can ............. 500.00-600.00

    Mickey Mouse tea set, w/2 chairs & small china set ..500.00-575.00

    Mickey Mouse (5¾") with two moveable arms ........... 500.00-550.00

    Mickey Mouse holding flag and sword ...................... 150.00-175.00

    Mickey Mouse (5¼") playing musical instruments .... 350.00-450.00

    Minnie Mouse (5") standing with hands on hips ........ 350.00-400.00

    Minnie Mouse holding nurse's kit .............................. 160.00-170.00

    Minnie Mouse (3½") pushing wheelbarrow ............... 400.00-425.00

    Minnie Mouse standing next to garbage can ............. 500.00-600.00

    Minnie Mouse (5¼") hands on hips .......................... 400.00-500.00

    Minnie Mouse with two moveable arms .................... 450.00-500.00

Blocks, wooden, Halsam Products Co. (set) ..................... 55.00-60.00

Bracelets, enameled metal, Cohn & Rosenberger ............. 65.00-75.00

Brush and Comb Sets, wood with enameled metal

    Hughes Co. (set) ......................................................... 75.00-85.00

Camera, British Ensign Ltd ........................................... 200.00-225.00

Candy Vendor Machine, with decal,

    Hamilton Co ....................................................... 1,500.00-1,600.00

Celluloid Wind Ups

    Pluto pulling Mickey Mouse in cart ..................... 2,000.00-2,100.00

    Mickey Mouse on tricycle ........................................ 750.00-800.00

    Mickey Mouse Mouse trapeze ................................... 450.00-500.00

    Horace Horsecollar pulling Mickey ................. 10,000.00-12,000.00

    Mickey Mouse walking Pluto ............................... 1,100.00-1,200.00

    Mickey Mouse whirlgig with celluloid characters ...3,300.00-3,400.00

    Mickey Mouse and Donald Duck trapeze ............. 2,000.00-2,200.00

    Mickey Mouse driving cart with 3 wheels ............. 2,000.00-2,100.00

    Mickey Mouse on elephant .................................. 3,500.00-4,000.00

Clock electric, Ingersoll .......................................... 900.00-1,000.00

Comb, American Hard Rubber Co ................................... 40.00-45.00

Cookie Box, cardboard .............................................. 175.00-200.00

Cookie Cutters, Aluminum Speciality Co .......................... 35.00-40.00

Cups, silver plated, International Silver Co ..................... 60.00-70.00

    China, Bavarian ......................................................... 70.00-75.00

Desk, wooden, child's Kroehler ................................... 250.00-300.00

Dishes, Beetleware, plastic, Bryant Elec. Co ..................... 20.00-25.00

Dolls

    Charlotte Clark Originals ..................................... 2,000.00-2,500.00

    Charlotte Clark McCall Pattern ................................. 300.00-325.00

    Dean's Rag Doll 14" ................................................ 500.00-550.00

    Dean's Safety-First Mickey .................................. 2,000.00-2,200.00

    Dean's Mickey Mouse Skater ............................... 2,500.00-3,000.00

    Knickerbocker Western Minnie Mouse ................. 3,000.00-3,500.00

    Knickerbocker Clown Mickey Mouse .................... 3,000.00-3,500.00

    Knickerbocker Two Gun Mickey Mouse with Chaps ... 650.00-675.00

    Steiff Mickey Mouse 5" ........................................ 750.00-900.00

    Steiff Minnie Mouse 9" ..................................... 1,200.00-1,400.00

Drum, tin lithograph, Ohio Art .................................... 300.00-325.00

Drummer, 7" metal, press lever and

    arms beat drum, Nifty Toy Co ........................... 2,500.00-3,000.00

Fishing Kit, metal lithograph, Hamilton Metal Products ...220.00-230.00

Flashlight, came with batteries, U.S. Electric Co ........... 300.00-325.00

Games

    Coming Home, Marks Bros. .................................... 135.00-140.00

    Scatterball, Marks ................................................ 120.00-130.00

    Globetrotters Bread Game with Map ......................... 200.00-225.00

    Mickey Mouse/Minnie Mouse ball game, Marks ........... 85.00-95.00

    Old Maid ................................................................ 20.00-30.00

    Mickey Mouse Party Game, Marks .............................. 40.00-45.00

    Target Game with gun, Marks .................................. 300.00-325.00

Horn, party, cardboard with metal mouthpiece ................. 75.00-80.00

Kite, paper, Marks Bros. ............................................... 60.00-70.00

Knife, pocketsize, Imperial Knife .................................. 90.00-95.00

Lamps, Mickey sitting in chair, Soreng Manegold ...2,400.00-2,500.00

    Tin base with decal, Soreng Manegold ...................... 100.00-105.00

Lantern Outfit, with full color slides, pistol shaped &

    battery operated projector, Ensign Ltd. ...................... 150.00-170.00

Lights, Christmas, complete set, Noma Electric Co ......200.00-215.00

Lunch Box, lithographed metal,

    Geuder Paeschke & Frey ..................................... 2,000.00-2,100.00

Magic Slate, used for jotting memos ............................... 25.00-30.00

Marionettes, wooden, Madame Alexander ..................... 400.00-450.00

Masks, paper, Einson-Freeman ...................................... 20.00-25.00

Milk Bottle, Libbey Glass Company .................................. 60.00-85.00

Napkin Ring, celluloid, plastic novelties .......................... 45.00-50.00

Pencil Box, figural, Dixon ......................................... 100.00-115.00

Pencil Sharpener, small, celluloid plastic novelties .......... 25.00-30.00

Phonograph, Emerson .......................................... 2,400.00-2,600.00

Piano, Mickey Mouse, Minnie Mouse Grand ................. 700.00-750.00

    Mickey Mouse, Minnie Mouse with dancing

    figures .............................................................. 1,500.00-1,800.00

Pitchers 6" creamer, Borgfeldt ...................................... 55.00-65.00

Popcorn Popper, "See'em Pop," Empire Products ......... 250.00-270.00

Projectors

    Movie Jektor ......................................................... 300.00-350.00

    Talkie Jektor ......................................................... 300.00-350.00

    Movie Projector, Keystone ....................................... 400.00-425.00

Pull Toys, wooden car, Borgfeldt, Nifty .......................... 300.00-350.00

Pluto pulling revolving Mickeys, N.N. Hill Brass Co. ......250.00-275.00

Mickey Mouse Wheelbarrow, Toy Kraft ........................ 150.00-175.00

Mickey Mouse hobby horse .............................................. 150.00-175.00
Puzzle, picture, Marks Bros. ...................................... 45.00-50.00
Racing Car, miniature car, Joseph Schneider Co. .......... 200.00-225.00
Radio, brown carved, Emerson ................................ 950.00-1,050.00
    White or black, has aluminum plate, Emerson .......... 875.00-925.00
Recipe Scrapbook, without recipes ................................... 70.00-75.00
    With recipes ................................................ 200.00-225.00
Rocking Horse, wooden, Mengel Co ............................ 250.00-300.00
Rolypoly, celluloid Mickey on top of ball, Borgfeldt ... 2,000.00-2,200.00
Rug, Alexander Smith & Sons Carpet Co. ...................... 225.00-235.00
Ruler, came in Dixon pencil box, 10" ............................... 20.00-25.00
Shovel, for sand pails, Ohio Art ........................................ 30.00-35.00
Sled, with complete decal, Slallen Co. .......................... 375.00-390.00
Sparkler, 5½" metal, Nifty Toy Co. .............................. 550.00-575.00
Stove, heavy metal, Metal Ware Corp. .......................... 275.00-300.00
Tea Set, complete china, George Borgfeldt .................. 300.00-325.00
    Tin lithograph, Ohio Art ........................................ 200.00-225.00
Thermometer, celluloid base, plastic novelties .............. 185.00-195.00
Tie Rack, wooden panel with illustrations ...................... 115.00-125.00
Toy Chest, heavy cardboard, Odora Co. ........................ 135.00-150.00
Tool Box with tools, Hamilton Metal Prod. .................... 140.00-145.00
Toothbrush, figural Mickey on handle, Hughes ............ 115.00-120.00
Trains
    Santa Mickey Mouse handcar, Lionel .................. 1,500.00-1,750.00
    Mickey Mouse Circus Train, complete with tent ... 4,500.00-5,000.00
    Mickey Mouse freight, Lionel ...................... 1,200.00-1,400.00
Tricycle, metal, Colson Company .......................... 1,000.00-1,100.00
Umbrella, figural handle, Louis Weiss ........................ 185.00-190.00
Wagon, Dayton Company ........................................ 160.00-175.00
Wall Plaques, wooden figural, Kerk Guild, Inc. ................ 40.00-45.00
Washer, 4½" x 7", childs, 3 metal legs, Ohio Art ............ 225.00-235.00
Watches
    Lapel Pin, came with a cord and button, Ingersoll .... 600.00-700.00
    Pocket Watch with fob, Ingersoll .............................. 500.00-525.00
Windups, metal, German, five-fingered Mickey Mouse, ratlike
    Mickey Mouse Slate Dancer ...................... 2,600.00-2,800.00
    Minnie Mouse pushing Felix the Cat .................. 5,000.00-5,500.00
    Mickey Mouse Paddleboat .............................. 4,000.00-4,500.0
    Mickey Mouse and Minnie Mouse
    organ grinder ............................................ 10,000.00-12,000.00

## Long-billed Donald Duck

Bisque Figures
    Donald Duck (1¾") hands on hips ................................ 50.00-55.00
    Donald Duck (3") with bill open .................................. 60.00-65.00
    Donald Duck holding flag ............................................ 60.00-65.00
    Donald Duck holding rifle ........................................ 160.00-165.00
    Donald Duck blowing bugle ...................................... 100.00-125.00
    Donald Duck sitting on rocking horse ...................... 220.00-250.00
    Donald Duck with two moveable arms ...................... 500.00-550.00
    Donald Duck holding paintbrush .............................. 600.00-625.00
    Donald Duck (4½") with musical instruments .......... 400.00-425.00
    Donald Duck (5¾") two moveable arms .................... 800.00-850.00
    Donald Duck toothbrush holder next to pillar .......... 700.00-725.00
    Donald Duck toothbrush holder with bill open ........ 250.00-275.00
Dolls, 12" with composition feet, Knickerbocker .......... 400.00-475.00
    Steiff, with button in ear ...................................... 1,300.00-1,500.00
Games
    Walt Disney's Own Donald Duck Party Game, Parker .... 50.00-55.00
    Bean Bag Party Game, Parker ...................................... 45.00-50.00
Hairbrush, enameled and wood, Hughes .......................... 45.00-50.00

Lamp, Donald Duck standing by pole,
    Soreng Manegold Co. ............................................ 2,400.00-2,500.00
    Tablelamp, metal base, Soreng Manegold Co .................. 75.00-85.00
Marionette, Madame Alexander ...................................... 350.00-375.00
Pencil Sharpener, celluloid, plastic novelties ................ 150.00-175.00
Rocking Horse, wooden ................................................ 250.00-275.00
Windups, celluloid
    Donald Duck trapeze ................................................ 600.00-625.00
    Mickey Mouse and Donald Duck trapeze .................. 800.00-825.00
    Donald Duck on elephant ...................................... 2,500.00-2,700.00
    Donald Duck on tricycle ............................................ 425.00-450.00
    Donald Duck whirligig .......................................... 2,500.00-2,800.00
    Donald Duck whirligig with characters ................ 3,500.00-4,000.00
Wooden Figures
    3" Borgfeldt .......................................................... 225.00-250.00
    5" Borgfeldt .......................................................... 400.00-425.00

## Snow White & Seven Dwarfs

Bagatelle, Chad Valley .................................................... 125.00-135.00
Banks, dime register ........................................................ 80.00-90.00
    Ceramic Dopey, Crown Toy Co. .................................. 85.00-95.00
Bracelet, charm, Larier Mfg. Co. .................................... 45.00-50.00
Bread Cards, recipes ........................................................ 20.00-25.00
Brooches, plastic with enameled metal, Brier Mfg. Co. ..... 40.00-45.00
Cards, playing, cardboard .............................................. 30.00-35.00
Carpet Sweeper, Musical, Fisher Price ............................ 95.00-105.00
Casting Set, iron, J.L. Wright .......................................... 70.00-80.00
Dolls
    Snow White, Madame Alexander .............................. 400.00-450.00
    Snow White, Ideal .................................................. 225.00-250.00
    Snow White, Knickerbocker .................................... 300.00-350.00
    Snow White, Krueger .............................................. 175.00-200.00
    Musical Dwarfs, Knickerbocker (each) ...................... 175.00-200.00
Games
    Snow White & 7 Dwarfs Target game,
    America Toy Works ................................................ 40.00-45.00
    Snow White moving target, Marks ............................ 130.00-140.00
    Skittles, Chad Valley .............................................. 20.00-25.00
    Dopey Bean Bag, Parker .......................................... 30.00-35.00
    Jack In The Box, Dopey, Marks Bros. ........................ 300.00-350.00
Masks, giveaways, Einson-Freeman ................................ 15.00-20.00
Ornaments, Christmas, 1930's ........................................ 150.00-175.00
Pencil Sharpeners, figural, celluloid .............................. 40.00-45.00
Perfume, child's toiletry figural bottles .......................... 100.00-110.00
Piano moving dwarfs, Marks Bros. ............................ 2,000.00-2,200.00
Pictures, framed in an antique manner, Aristo Inc. ......... 15.00-20.00
Radio, wooden with colorful dwarfs ............................ 2,200.00-2,400.00
Sandpail, lithographed metal, Ohio Art Co. .................... 60.00-65.00
Spoon, baby, silver, International Silver Co. .................... 30.00-35.00
Tea Set, china, Borgfeldt ................................................ 250.00-275.00
    Lithographed metal, Ohio ........................................ 175.00-200.00
Tie Rack, wooden .......................................................... 40.00-45.00
Toothbrush Holder, glazed ceramic, Borgfeldt .............. 100.00-115.00
Valentine, mechanical, Dopey ........................................ 20.00-25.00

## Three Little Pigs

Dolls
    Big Bad Wolf, Krueger .............................................. 70.00-75.00
Game, Who's Afraid of the Big Bad Wolf,
    Einson-Freeman ...................................................... 50.00-55.00
Jewelry, made of gold & platinum, Philip Reiter ............ 35.00-40.00

Picture, color set, Bates Art Ind. ........................20.00-25.00
Picture Set, complete, Arti-Stamp .......................30.00-35.00
Rubber, Latex (all 3 pigs), Seiberling .............900.00-1,000.00
    Big Bad Wolf ...........................................550.00
Silverware Set, International Silver Co. ...................75.00-80.00
Snapshots, picture album, Richard Krueger Co. .............35.00-40.00
Watch, pocket watch with fob, Ingersoll ...............850.00-900.00
Wind up, Schuco ..........................................150.00-175.00
Wooden Toys, Fun-E-Flex (all 3), Borgfeldt ............400.00-425.00

## Pinocchio

Bank, wood pulp, composition,
    Crown Manufacturing Co. ...........................175.00-180.00
Candles, wax, Manhattan Wax Candle Co. ...............30.00-35.00
Game, Pinocchio the Merry Puppet, Milton Bradley ........50.00-55.00
Glasses, 12 in set, Owens Illinois (set) ..............100.00-120.00
Lamps, wall and table, made of wood fiber,
    Flexo Products ......................................100.00-110.00
Masks, Gillette giveaway, paper ........................15.00-20.00
Windup, walker, tin lithograph, Marx ...................200.00-225.00
Wooden
    19" Ideal .............................................600.00-625.00
    12" Ideal .............................................350.00-400.00
    10" Ideal .............................................200.00-225.00
    Mechanical 10½" tall, Borgfeldt ....................600.00-650.00
    5" Fun-E-Flex, Borgfeldt ...........................100.00-110.00
Wood Fiber, molded wood, Multi Products .................50.00-55.00

## Modern Day

American Pottery Company
    Bambi with butterfly ...............................70.00-80.00
    Mickey Mouse .......................................100.00-125.00
    Minnie Mouse .......................................100.00-125.00
    Donald Duck ........................................100.00-125.00
    Pluto ..............................................60.00-70.00
    Snow White .........................................120.00-130.00
    Pinocchio ..........................................50.00-60.00
    Jiminy Cricket .....................................50.00-60.00
Bed Spreads, Colorama Inc. ..............................20.00-25.00
Binoculars, plastic, Royal American Corp. ................10.00-15.00
Brayton's Laguna Pottery
    Donald Duck on left elbow ..........................75.00-100.00
    Snow White .........................................350.00-400.00
    Seven Dwarfs (each) ................................80.00-90.00
    Pluto, howling .....................................80.00-90.00
    Figaro, begging ....................................60.00-70.00
    Jiminy Cricket with hand on hip ....................50.00-60.00
    Squawking Donald Duck ..............................85.00-95.00
    Pinocchio on knee of Geppetto ......................350.00-400.00
    Pinocchio with apple ...............................80.00-90.00
Brushes, Hughes Autograph Brush Co. .....................15.00-20.00
    Sterling, Am Metalcrafts ...........................20.00-25.00
Camera, Donald Duck, plastic Herbert George Co. .........35.00-40.00
Cookie Jars, Leeds China Company ........................50.00-65.00
Disneyland
    Nursey Tea Set, Beswick ............................150.00-175.00
    Projector 1950's ...................................50.00-60.00
    Roller Coaster, Chein ..............................200.00-225.00
    Ferris Wheel, Chein ................................300.00-350.00
    Melody Player, hand operated .......................125.00-135.00
    Disneyland Game, Transogram ........................20.00-25.00

Mickey Mouse Club Game in Disneyland, Whitman ......15.00-20.00
    Fantasyland Game, Parker ...........................15.00-20.00
Dolls (Contemporary)
    Mickey Mouse, Gund .................................50.00-60.00
    Donald Duck, Gund ..................................50.00-60.00
    Pluto, Gund ........................................45.00-50.00
    Dumbo, Gund ........................................70.00-80.00
    Mickey Mouse, Sun Rubber ...........................10.00-12.00
Dresser Set, translucent pastel plastic,
    Herbert George Company .............................10.00-15.00
Friction Toys
    Donald Duck's Rocket ...............................200.00-225.00
    Donald Duck Motorcycle, Line-Mar ...................200.00-225.00
    Mickey Mouse racing car, Marx ......................225.00-250.00
    Fun on Wheels, Empire Toys .........................15.00-18.00
Gumball Machine, Hasbro .................................10.00-12.00
Hagen-Renaker Ceramics
    Bambi ..............................................150.00-175.00
    Thumper ............................................80.00-90.00
    Mickey Mouse, the band leader ......................140.00-150.00
    Tramp ..............................................120.00-130.00
    Peg ................................................120.00-130.00
    Alice ..............................................125.00-135.00
    Pluto ..............................................140.00-150.00
    Goofy ..............................................130.00-140.00
    Donald Duck ........................................120.00-130.00
    Gus or Jaq .........................................80.00-85.00
    Scrooge McDuck .....................................100.00-110.00
    Snow White .........................................95.00-105.00
    Maleficent and Raven ...............................500.00-525.00
Jack in the Box, CBS Toys ...............................10.00-12.00
Knife, pocket, Davy Crockett Frontier ...................20.00-25.00
Lamps, wall and table, all characters, Railley Co. .......60.00-65.00
Leeds China
    Figures ............................................30.00-35.00
    Planters ...........................................35 00-45.00
    Child's Feeding Dishes .............................45.00-50.00
Library of Card Games, Russel Manufacturing .............25.00-30.00
Lunch Boxes
    Pinocchio, Libbey ..................................30.00-35.00
    Davy Crocket, Liberty ..............................20.00-25.00
    Disney Fire Engine .................................10.00-15.00
Mickey Mouse Club
    Explorers Club Outfit, L.M. Eddy ...................60.00-65.00
    Mickey Mouse Club Projector, Stephens ..............40.00-45.00
    Medical Kit, with instruments ......................25.00-30.00
    Mickey Mouse Club Circus, True-Vue .................25.00-30.00
    Fan Club Typewriter, tin lithograph ................50.00-55.00
    Mouseketeer badge ..................................10.00-15.00
    Mouse Getar Jr. ....................................45.00-50.00
    Soaky Bottle .......................................15.00-20.00
Pencil Box, Hasbro ......................................20.00-25.00
Pull Toys, Fisher Price
    Donald Duck Baton Twirler ..........................150.00-175.00
    Donald Duck Wagon ..................................90.00-100.00
    Donald Duck Xylophone ..............................200.00-210.00
    Donald Duck 19" tall, movable arms & legs ..........220.00-230.00
    Donald Duck & his nephews ..........................175.00-200.00
    Donald Duck Drummer ................................125.00-150.00
    Donald Duck Drum Major .............................150.00-160.00
    Talking Donald (plastic feet) ......................40.00-45.00

Doc & Dopey Dwarfs ................................................ 180.00-185.00
Mickey Mouse Puddle Jumper ........................................ 40.00-45.00
Mickey Mouse Xylophone ........................................... 100.00-125.00
Mickey Mouse Drummer ............................................. 90.00-100.00
Mickey Mouse Safety Patrol ........................................ 160.00-170.00
Plucky Pinocchio .................................................. 160.00-170.00
Puzzles, wooden inlay, Judy Co. ................................... 10.00-15.00
    Jigsaw, Jaymar Speciality Co. ............................. 15.00-20.00
Radio, plastic Mickey Mouse lying on top .......................... 25.00-30.00
Salt and Pepper shakers, ceramic .................................. 25.00-30.00
Scissors, electric, Royal American ................................ 15.00-20.00
Shooting Gallery, Lido, 1950s ..................................... 25.00-30.00
Sink, Snow White, metal, Wolverine ................................ 30.00-35.00
Soap, character, 48 Disney characters,
    Monogram Soap Co. ........................................ 10.00-15.00
Squeeze Toys, Dell ................................................ 12.00-15.00
Stoves, Snow White, metal Wolverine ............................... 30.00-35.00
Television Play House, Marx Playset ............................... 75.00-100.00
Top, tin lithograph, Chein ........................................ 15.00-20.00
Trains
    Disneyland train, metal locomotive, Marx ................. 50.00-60.00
    Casey Jr., Marx .......................................... 30.00-35.00
    Mickey Mouse Meteor, Line-Mar ........................... 300.00-350.00
Watches
    Cinderella wristwatch, U.S. Time ......................... 40.00-45.00
    Davy Crockett, wristwatch, U.S. Time ..................... 50.00-55.00
    Snow White, wristwatch, U.S. Time ........................ 40.00-45.00
    Mickey Mouse, Timex electric, 1970 ...................... 250.00-275.00
    Donald Duck, wristwatch, U.S. Time ....................... 70.00-75.00
    Railroad pocket watch, Elgin ............................. 40.00-45.00
Wind Up Toys
    Donald Duck Duet, Marx .................................. 600.00-625.00
    Mickey Mouse Express, Marx .............................. 350.00-400.00
    Mickey Mouse Acrobat, Line-Mar .......................... 375.00-400.00
    Disney Parade Roadster, Marx ............................ 350.00-400.00
    Donald Duck the Skier, Marx ............................. 300.00-325.00
    Donald Duck the Drummer, Marx ........................... 300.00-325.00
    Donald Duck, Mavco ...................................... 125.00-150.00
    Mickey Mouse Crazy Car, Line-Mar ........................ 275.00-300.00
    Climbing Fireman Donald ................................. 350.00-400.00
    Minnie Mouse Rocker, Line-Mar ........................... 500.00-550.00
    Mickey Mouse on Unicycle, Line-Mar ...................... 850.00-900.00
    Mechanical Goofy with rotating tail ..................... 175.00-200.00
    Mickey Mouse with rotating tail, Marx ................... 175.00-200.00
    Mickey Mouse's Disney Jalopy, Line-Mar .................. 175.00-200.00
    Donald Crazy Car ........................................ 325.00-350.00
    Pinocchio the Acrobat ................................... 275.00-300.00
    Roll Over Pluto, Marx ................................... 200.00-225.00
    Goofy the Gardener, Marx ................................ 500.00-525.00
    Mickey Mouse on Skates .................................. 850.00-900.00
    Mickey Mouse Skooter, Marco ............................. 150.00-175.00

### Disney Buttons

Mickey Mouse Book Club, 1970's .................................... 10.00
Country Mickey Mouse Club, 1930's ................................. 85.00
Mickey Mouse Undies, 1928-1930 .................................... 65.00
Minnie Mouse, 1940's .............................................. 18.00
Happy Birthday Mickey 1928-1978 ................................... 15.00
Mickey Mouse Springle-Bell-Chick Ok, 1930's ...................... 80.00
Mickey From Fantasia .............................................. 7.00
Mickey's 1935 Birthday Button ..................................... 100.00

Member Mickey Mouse Globetrotters ................................ 35.00
Mickey Mouse Club KVOS-TV12, 1950's .............................. 25.00
Mirth Mickey Mouse Club 1928-1930 ................................ 65.00
I Grew Up On Mickey Mouse, 1970's ................................ 10.00
Mickey Mouse Club 1928-1930 ...................................... 75.00
Mickey Mouse Good Teeth .......................................... 75.00
Mickey & Co., 1980's ............................................. 5.00
Walt Disney's Dumbo, 1941 ........................................ 18.00
Zorro - 7 Up, 1957 ............................................... 30.00
Walt Disney's Pinocchio, 1940 .................................... 25.00
Disneyland 25 Meet Me at the Family Reunion, 1980 ................ 8.00
Pennies for Back to School, 1930's ............................... 40.00
The Detroit News - 1979 Disney World Winner ..................... 15.00
Jiminy Cricket, I'm No Fool About Safety, 1950's ................. 18.00
Member Snow White Jingle Club, 1938 .............................. 25.00
Disneyland 1966 Tiger Frolics .................................... 20.00
Disneyland 1966 Bi-Centennial .................................... 20.00
Walt Disney's Dumbo D-X, 1942 .................................... 25.00
Happy Birthday Donald Duck 1934-1984 ............................. 3.00
Walt Disney's Snow White, 1938 ................................... 300.00
Dumbo the Flying Elephant, 1960's ................................ 10.00
Bongo the Circus Performing Bear, 1960's ......................... 10.00
Hippy the Hippo, 1960's .......................................... 10.00
I'm Goofy About Disneyland, 1960's ............................... 10.00
I like Disneyland, 1960's ........................................ 10.00
I like Walt Disney World, 1970 ................................... 5.00
Disney On Parade ................................................. 5.00
Davy Crockett Frontiersman, 1950's ............................... 25.00
The Disney Channel, 1981 ......................................... 10.00
Disneyland Directors Guild of America Day 1983 ................... 20.00
Eat Frihofer's Perfect Loaf, 1930's .............................. 25.00
Hi Diddle Dee Pinocchio, 1940 .................................... 35.00
I'm A Fire Safety Expert, 1984 ................................... 5.00
Disneyland ....................................................... 25.00
Disneyland's 25th Birthday Party 1980 ............................ 5.00
Disneyland's 30th Year 1985 ...................................... 5.00
The Disney Channel 1982 .......................................... 5.00
Donna Duck, 1980 ................................................. 5.00
Disneyland at Selfridges, 1970's ................................. 5.00
Disney on Parade, 1970's ......................................... 8.00
The Aristocats From Walt Disney Productions ...................... 12.00
The Rescuers at Selfridges, 1970 ................................. 5.00
Rescuers, 1970's ................................................. 5.00
Bambi, 1950's .................................................... 20.00
Who's Afraid of the Big Bad Wolf, 1935 ........................... 85.00
Donald Duck Jackets .............................................. 250.00
Fess Parker as Davy Crockett ..................................... 25.00
Rabbit ........................................................... 10.00
Tigger ........................................................... 10.00

### Bambi

Bambi, large ceramic figure 4" x6" x8½", 1949, Evan K Shaw ... 135.00
Wise Owl, American Pottery, 1949 ................................. 200.00
Bambi butterfly, 1½" x 2" x 2¾", 1949, American Pottery ......... 195.00
Bambi with butterfly, 3½" x 7" x 8", 1947, American Pottery .... 200.00
Flower, glazed ceramic, 1" x 2" x1½", 1956, Shaw ................ 150.00
Thumper, Miniature, ceramic, 1956, Shaw ......................... 125.00
Bambi Soaky Bottle, 1960's ....................................... 12.00
Thumper, rubber, 1940's, Sun Rubber Co. .......................... 28.00
Bambi Planter, 1940's, 5" x 10" x 6" ............................. 25.00
Sheet Music, "Love is a Song", 1942 ............................. 18.00

Flower Friction Toy, 1960's, Line-mar ............................... 14.00
Bambi, ceramic figurine, 1950's, Goebel ......................... 100.00
Bambi China Ashtray, 1950's, 3½" x 3" ........................... 125.00
Thumper Cookie Jar, 1940's .............................................. 40.00
Bambi Ceramic Vase ........................................................ 12.00
Thumper Ceramic Planter ................................................ 25.00
Bambi "Glow in the Dark" Framed Pictures ..................... 18.00
Thumper Salt & Pepper Set, 1940's ................................ 18.00
Flower, Ceramic 2½" x 3" x 4½", 1940's, American Pottery ......... 45.00
Bambi Plastic Picture Game ............................................... 7.00
Bambi Doll, Steiff, 1½" x5" x5½" ....................................... 75.00
Bambi Wall Planter, glazed china .................................... 20.00
Bambi Alarm Clock, 1972, Bayard ................................. 200.00
Thumper Soaky Bottle ...................................................... 12.00
Bambi Doll, large, 5" x 11" x 15", Gund .......................... 70.00
Bambi die-cut and wood composition, 1942 ................... 30.00
Thumper, glazed ceramic, 3" x 3½" x4", American Pottery ......... 50.00
Flower, ceramic, 4½", 1942, American Pottery ................ 70.00
Thumper, ceramic, 4" , 1941, American Pottery ............. 60.00
Thumper & Girlfriend Glow in the Dark Picture .............. 18.00
Flower Chalk Bank, 1940's ............................................. 35.00
Bambi Doll, Character Novelty Co, 1940's ...................... 25.00
Thumper Figural Ashtray, Goebel, 1950's ..................... 175.00
Bambi Puzzle, Jaymar ..................................................... 20.00
"Bambi as told by Shirley Temple" record, RCA 78 RMP ......... 30.00

### Mary Poppins

Carousel Game, 1964, Parker Brothers ........................... 15.00
Disneyland Record, 45 RMP .............................................. 10.00
Figure, China, 3" x 3½" x 8", 1964 .................................. 12.00
Spoon, 1964, Wm. Rogers ............................................... 10.00
Frame Tray Puzzle, 1964, Whitman ................................. 12.00
Easel, Stand Up, 1964 ..................................................... 10.00
Hand Puppet, 11", 1960's, Sweldin .................................. 12.00

### Davy Crockett

Alamo Play Set No. 3540, Marx ...................................... 300.00
Alamo Construction Set, 1955, Practi-Cole Products ...... 175.00
Tie Bar & Cuff Link Set, 1955 .......................................... 27.00
Official Powder Horn, 1955 .............................................. 65.00
Cereal Bowl ..................................................................... 10.00
Ceramic Mug .................................................................... 10.00
Watch, U.S. Time, 1950's ................................................. 60.00
Stampbook #1, 32 pages .................................................. 35.00
Puzzles, 1950's, Jaymar .................................................. 18.00
Walt Disney's Official Davy Crockett Alamo, Marx ......... 50.00
Walt Disney's Frontierland Davy Crockett Outfit, 1955 .............. 35.00
Lunch Box, 1955, Aladdin ................................................ 37.00
Record, "The Three Adventures of Davy Crockett," 33 RMP, 1955 ... 15.00
Marx Playset Figure, 2" plastic ....................................... 15.00
Official Souvenir Song Book, 1955 .................................. 15.00
Walt Disney's Official Frontierland Pencil Case, 1956 .............. 35.00
Davy Crockett Thermos, 8½", 1955 ............................... 12 .00
Davy Crockett/Fess Parker Girl's Play Suit ..................... 22.00
"Indian Attack" Jigsaw Puzzle ......................................... 20.00

### Ferdinand

Glazed Ceramic Figure, 1938, Vernon Kiln .................... 95.00
Carnival Figure, plaster ................................................... 30.00
Bisque Figurine, 1¾", 1930's .......................................... 30.00
Pillow Cover, 17" x 17", velvet-like cloth ........................ 30.00

Glazed china salt & pepper shakers, 1938 .................... 33.00
Ferdinand "Mama" Glass, 1938, WDE ............................ 22.00
Ferdinand "The Bee" Glass, 1938, WDE .......................... 22.00

### Dumbo

Figurine, ceramic, 3½" x 4" x 4", Goebel ...................... 325.00
Doll, plush, 1949, Gund .................................................. 40.00
Record, 1948, RCA Victor ................................................ 23.00
Fun mask, Wheaties, 1950's ............................................ 13.00
Salt and Pepper Shakers, ceramic, 4" ............................ 25.00
Premium "Flasher Disc," 1960's ....................................... 7.00
Figural Cream Pitcher, 6" tall .......................................... 30.00
Figurine, ceramic, 3" x 4" x 3½", Shaw ........................ 175.00
Double Cookie Jar, 1940's .............................................. 65.00
Ceramic Figure, 4" x 6" x 5½", Am. Pottery .................. 125.00
Ceramic Figure, 3" x 5" x 3½", Vernon Kiln #4 ............. 225.00
China Figure, 2" x 2½" ...................................................... 5.00
Dumbo Figural Squirt Gun, 1960's .................................... 8.00
Glazed Ceramic, 4½" x 5" x5½", 1946 .......................... 150.00
Composition Figure, movable head & trunk, Cameo Doll Prod. ... 150.00
Miniature Ceramic, l" x 1½" x 1½", 1970's .................... 15.00
Wall Plaque, wood .......................................................... 20.00
Pitcher, china, Leed's ...................................................... 55.00
Small glazed ceramic, l" x 2" x 2", 1940's .................... 35.00
"Dumbo at the Circus" blocks, Gatso Mfg. ..................... 25.00

### Cinderella

Picture Puzzle, 1950, Whitman ........................................ 21.00
Sheet Music, "Bibbidi-Bobbidi-Boo" ................................ 10.00
Glasses, 1940's, 4¾" ...................................................... 12.00
Planter, glazed china ....................................................... 23.00
Wall Plaque Set, 1951 ..................................................... 20.00
Slipper, clear plastic ........................................................ 12.00
Watch, 1950, U.S. Time ................................................... 35.00
Bank, 6", glazed china, 1950's ........................................ 33.00
Game, "Walt Disney's Cinderella", 1950, Parker Brothers ......... 22.00
Pendant, molded plastic, 1960's ..................................... 10.00
Record, "Four Songs From Cinderella" ............................ 10.00
Ceramic, Coachman, pastel, 1950, 2½" x 6" .................. 95.00
Glass, dairy, 1950's ......................................................... 10.00
Wind-up, plastic, 1950's .................................................. 80.00
Wind-up, plastic, dancing with Prince, Irwin ................. 105.00
Soaky Bottle, 1960's ........................................................ 15.00
Fun Mask, Wheaties ........................................................ 10.00
Frame Tray Puzzle, 10" x 13", 1950's ............................. 17.00
Record, "Cinderella Mickey Mouse Club" ....................... 15.00

### Alice in Wonderland

Stationery, Whitman ......................................................... 20.00
Planter, ceramic, 1940's .................................................. 55.00
Doll, Effanbee ................................................................. 50.00
Bank, glazed ceramic ...................................................... 35.00
Mug, china, 1970's .......................................................... 10.00
Salt & Pepper Set, 1950's ............................................... 22.00
Mad Hatter, glazed china, 4", American Pottery ........... 120.00
White Rabbit, glazed china, 3", American Pottery ......... 120.00
Figurine, ceramic, Japan ................................................. 12.00
White Rabbit Ceramic Creamer, 1950's ........................ 150.00
Sheet Music, "I'm Late," 1951 ......................................... 13.00
Marionette, 14" composition, Peter Puppet Plaything, 1950's ... 125.00
Alice and the Bottle Toy, plastic with wheels, 1950's .............. 18.00

Marionette, March Hare, 12" composition, 1951 ...........................85.00
Marionette, Mad Hatter, comp., wood, fabric, Peter Puppet ......150.00
Jar, White Rabbit, ceramic, head removable ...............................175.00

### Zorro

Official Shooting Outfit, 1960 ..............................................75.00
Lunchbox, with thermos, Aladdin .......................................35.00
Wrist Flashlight, 1960's ......................................................25.00
Wrist Watch, 1960's, U.S. Time ..........................................45.00
Pin Wheel ...........................................................................8.00
Mask, whip, ring, lariat set, Shimmel Sons .........................20.00
Target Set, 1960, Lido ........................................................20.00
Target Set, tin litho, darts, rifle, Cohn ...............................100.00
Billfold, plastic, 1960 .........................................................15.00
Puzzle, 1950's, Jaymar .......................................................20.00
Viewmaster, 3-reel set, 1958 ..............................................18.00
Zorro on horseback, 1950's .................................................18.00
Hat, 10½" x 3½", black plastic, 1950's ...............................20.00
Record, "Songs About Zorro & Other TV Heroes, 1960 .............12.00
Zorro game, boxed, 1965, Whitman ....................................15.00
Hand Puppet, 10", Gund ....................................................18.00
Mask, 1950's .....................................................................15.00
Zorro Equipment Set, M. Shimmel Sons .............................30.00
Flashlight, 3" pocket ..........................................................12.00

### Winnie the Pooh

Pooh Lamp & Wind up Music Box ......................................30.00
Game, Pooh, Robin, Piglet, Rabbit as playing pieces ...................15.00
Pooh, rubber squeeze toy ....................................................8.00
Cookie Jar, Pooh eating toy ................................................35.00
Ceramic Pooh holding pot of honey ....................................30.00
Bisque figure, Pooh with weather balloon, 1964 ........................23.00
Pooh's Honey Bank, glazed china, 1964 ..............................15.00

### Jiminy Cricket

Safety First Card Game, 1950's ..........................................15.00
Doll, jointed composition doll, Knickerbocker ....................325.00
Car, Matchbox ...................................................................10.00
Porcelain, 3½", 1939, National Porcelain Co. ......................25.00
Frame, white plastic, 1966 .................................................15.00
Glass, clear drinking, 1939 ................................................23.00
Mug, 4", plastic, 1960's ......................................................10.00
Figure, 4½", wood, composition, Multi Products .......................25.00

### Figaro

Drinking Glass ...................................................................15.00
Bisque Figure .....................................................................25.00
Pressed Wood Figure, 2" x 2" ..............................................30.00
Light green glazed porcelain figure .....................................15.00
China Planter, 1939 ...........................................................75.00
China Figure, 1940, 1½" x 2" x 2½" .....................................20.00

### Peter Pan

Bread Labels, 1950's ..........................................................18.00
Wall Plaques, wooden, 1952 ...............................................20.00
Bookbag, canvas, 1952 .......................................................20.00
"Game of Adventure," 1953, Transogram ............................22.00
Figure, Blue Vinyl, 6½", 1972, Marx ...................................14.00
Picture, cardboard in plastic frame, 1953 ...........................18.00
Marionette, Captain Hook, 15" wood & composition, 1953 .......105.00
Game, "Walt Disney's Peter Pan – A Game of Adventure,"

1953, Transogram ..............................................................23.00
Doll, Jointed, 11½", vinyl & plastic ....................................15.00
Bell, Tinkerbell Disneyland Souvenir, 1950's .....................20.00
Doll, 10", Sun Rubber ........................................................38.00
Puzzles, picture, 1952, Whitman ........................................45.00
Figure, Tinkerbell glazed china, 1960's ..............................10.00
Figure, 9½", 1950's, Sun Rubber .........................................22.00
Hat, bread premium, 1950's ...............................................18.00
Tru-Vue Film Card, 1954 ...................................................10.00
Puzzle Frame Tray, 1952, Whitman ....................................15.00
Rain Jacket, 1950's .............................................................18.00
Puppet, 9", Gund ...............................................................15.00

### Other Disney

Swiss Family Robinson Golden Record ...............................10.00
Jungle Book Lunch Box & Thermos, Aladdin .......................15.00
Jungle Book Bank, composition, 1955 .................................17.00
Gus Squeaky Toy ..................................................................5.00
Robin Hood Game, 1973, Parker Brothers ...........................15.00
Sword in the Stone Frame Tray Puzzle .................................12.00
Uncle Remus "Zip" Game ...................................................35.00
Tortoise and the Hare Puzzle, Jaymar .................................25.00
"The Three Caballeros" record album, 1944 ........................20.00
Donald-Jose Carioca Cookie Jar .........................................65.00
Sleeping Beauty paint with water, Whitman ........................35.00
Sleeping Beauty Magic Bubble Wand ..................................15.00
Babes in Toyland Game, 1961, Parker Brothers ...................20.00
Babes in Toyland doll, Gund ...............................................20.00
Babes in Toyland soldiers, Marx .........................................25.00
Annette's Secret Passage Game, 1958, Parker Brothers ............25.00
Shaggy Dog, 9" hand puppet, 1950's, Gund ........................15.00
Lady Doll, 1955, Gund ........................................................20.00
Lady Ceramic Figure, Wade of England ...............................10.00
Lady & the Tramp Original Cast Album, Capitol Records, 1954 ...20.00
Lady & the Tramp fiberboard picture, 1950's .......................20.00
101 Dalmatians Game, 1979, Whitman ...............................12.00
101 Dalmatians tall glazed ceramic figure, 1961 .................15.00
101 Dalmatians Puzzle 11" x 14", Jaymar ...........................10.00
Walt Disney's Treasure Island Record Set, 1950's ................27.00
101 Dalmatians 6½" Squeak Toy, vinyl ...............................15.00
101 Dalmatians china figure 2½" x 2" .................................12.00
Johnny Tremain and Horse, 1957, Marx ..............................65.00
Flora Hand Puppet, Gund ...................................................15.00
Westward Ho the Wagons Record ..........................................5.00
Brer Rabbit and Tar Baby Record, 45RPM, Capitol ................10.00
Sleeping Beauty Game, Parker Brothers ..............................10.00
Tramp Plush Doll, Gund .....................................................15.00
Tramp, 3" ceramic, Goebel .................................................25.00
Aristocats, glazed ceramic, 1968 ........................................18.00
Fantasia Elephant Figure, 2¼" x 2½" x 5", American Pottery ....175.00
Pecos Bill, windup, 1948, Marx .........................................175.00
20,000 Leagues Under the Sea Puzzle ..................................18.00
Lady glazed china figure, 1960s .........................................18.00
Lady & the Tramp Jigsaw Puzzle ........................................10.00
Hardy Boys Treasure Game, 1957, Parker Brothers ..............15.00

### Grosset & Dunlap

1936  Donald Duck ............................................................75.00
1937  Pluto the Puppy ........................................................50.00
1938  Snow White and Seven Dwarfs ..................................25.00
1939  Walt Disney's Version of Pinocchio ...........................75.00

1940 The Sorcerer's Apprentice .................................25.00
1942 Walt Disney's Thumper ....................................20.00
1943 Walt Disney's Pedro ........................................15.00
1943 Donald Duck in the High Andes ........................15.00
1946 The Wonderful Tar Baby ...................................12.00
1947 Mickey and the Beanstalk .................................12.00
1948 Come Play with Donald Duck .............................10.00
1948 Come Play with Mickey Mouse ...........................10.00
1949 Magnificent Mr. Toad ......................................12.00

### Saalfield
1931 Mickey Mouse Pictures to Paint ........................85.00
1931 Mickey Mouse Coloring Book ............................65.00
1932 Flip the Frog Coloring Book – your movie star .......75.00
1933 Mickey & Minnie Mouse Coloring Book ...............65.00
1935 Another Mickey Mouse Coloring Book ................75.00
1936 Mickey Mouse Book for Coloring .......................65.00
1967 Walt Disney Presents the Happiest Millionaire
       Coloring Book .............................................10.00

### D.D. Heath
#### Hardcover School Readers, published 1939-1940
Little Pigs' Picnic and other stories .......................25.00
Here They Are ...............................................20.00
Donald Duck and His Friends .............................20.00
Mickey Never Fails ..........................................25.00
School Days in Disneyville ................................25.00
Mickey Sees the USA .......................................25.00
Donald Duck Sees South America .......................25.00
Water Babies and Other Stories ..........................20.00
Walt Disney's Pinocchio ...................................20.00
Donald Duck and his Nephews ...........................20.00

### Whitman
#### (Big Little Books)
1933 Mickey Mouse #717 (lst) .............................130.00
1933 Mickey Mouse The Mailpilot ..........................40.00
1933 Mickey Mouse Sails for Treasure Island ............40.00
1934 Mickey Mouse in Blaggard Castle ...................35.00
1934 Mickey Mouse Presents a Walt Disney Silly Symphony .....35.00
1934 Mickey Mouse The Detective ..........................30.00
1935 Mickey Mouse and the Bat Bandit ...................30.00
1935 Mickey Mouse and Bobo the Elephant ..............35.00
1936 Mickey Mouse and the Sacred Jewel ................30.00
1936 Mickey Mouse Presents
       Walt Disney's Silly Symphonies Stories ............50.00
1936 Mickey Mouse and Pluto the Racer ..................25.00
1937 Silly Symphony Featuring Donald Duck .............50.00
1937 Mickey Mouse Runs His Own Newspaper ...........25.00
1937 Silly Symphony Featuring
       Donald Duck and His Misadventures ...............30.00
1938 Snow White and the Seven Dwarfs ..................35.00
1938 Pluto the Pup ............................................20.00
1938 Mickey Mouse in the Race for Riches ...............25.00
1938 Donald Duck Hunting for Trouble ...................20.00

### Whitman
#### (Better Little Books)
Walt Disney's Dumbo, #1400 ............................15.00
Mickey Mouse in the Treasure Hunt, # 1401 ..........20.00
Ghost Morgan's Treasure, #1411 .......................20.00

Mickey Mouse and the 'Lectro Box', #1413 ............20.00
Mickey Mouse on Sky Island, #1417 ...................20.00
Donald Duck Sees Stars, #1422 ........................25.00
Donald Duck Says Such Luck, #1424 ..................20.00
Mickey Mouse in the Foreign Legion, #1428 ..........20.00
Mickey Mouse and the Magic Lamp, #1429 ...........18.00
Donald Duck-Headed for Trouble, #1430 .............20.00
Donald Duck and the Green Serpent, #1432 ..........18.00
Walt Disney's Pinocchio and Jiminy Cricket, #1435 ...15.00
Donald Duck Off the Beam, #1438 .....................15.00
Mickey Mouse in the World of Tomorrow, #1441 .....18.00
Donald Duck Lays Down the Law, #1449 ..............18.00
Mickey Mouse and the Desert Place, #1451 ..........18.00
Donald Duck in Volcano Valley, #1457 ................15.00
Donald Duck Gets Fed Up, #1462 .....................15.00
Mickey Mouse and the Pirate Submarine, #1463 .....18.00
Mickey Mouse and the Dude Ranch Bandit, #1471 ...18.00
Mickey Mouse and the 7 Ghosts, #1475 ..............18.00
Mickey Mouse in the Race for Riches, #1476 .........15.00
Such a Life! Says: Donald Duck, #1484 ...............25.00
Donald Duck-Up in the Air, #1486 ....................15.00
Mickey Mouse on the Cave-Man Island, #1499 ......15.00

### Dell
1938 Walt Disney's Ferdinand the Bull (soft cover) .....25.00
1938 Mickey Mouse with Goofy & Mickey's Nephews .....70.00
1938 Mickey Mouse the Sheriff of Nugget Gulch ........70.00
1941 Walt Disney's Donald Duck Takes It on the Chin ...25.00
1941 Walt Disney's Dumbo the Flying Elephant .........20.00
1941 So Dear To My Heart –
       The Story of the Walt Disney Picture ..............20.00
1954 Walt Disney's Coloring Book .........................12.00
1959 Shaggy Dog Coloring Book ............................8.00

### Whitman
#### (Wee Little Books, 3" x 3½", 1934)
Mickey Mouse Will Not Quit ..............................20.00
Mickey Mouse's Uphill Fight .............................20.00
Mickey Mouse's Misfortune ..............................20.00
Mickey Mouse and Tanglefoot ...........................20.00
Mickey Mouse at the Carnival ...........................20.00
Mickey Mouse Wins the Race ............................20.00

### Whitman
1934 Mickey Mouse Presents a
       Walt Disney Symphony Book to Color ..............75.00
1935 Walt Disney's Donald Duck ..........................250.00
1935 The Big Book – The Story of Mickey Mouse ........75.00
1936 Draw and Paint Donald Duck ........................45.00
1936 A Mickey Mouse ABC, Story by Walt Disney ......150.00
1936 Mickey Mouse in Pigmyland ..........................75.00
1936 Walt Disney Presents 40 Big Pages of Mickey Mouse ...55.00
1936 Mickey Mouse and Pluto the Pup ...................45.00
1936 Mickey Mouse and His Friends (linen) ..............225.00
1936 Forty Big Pages of Mickey Mouse ...................75.00
1937 Donald Duck Debuts in the "Wise Little Hen" ......110.00
1937 Mickey's Magic Hat Cookie Carnival ................75.00
1937 Mickey Mouse Presents Walt Disney's Nursery Stories ...125.00
1937 Donald Duck Story Book .............................100.00
1938 Walt Disney's Clock Cleaners ........................55.00
1938 Mickey Mouse Has a Party ...........................35.00

1938 Ferdinand the Bull (linen-like) ............................25.00
1938 Snow White and Seven Dwarfs Paper Dolls ....................80.00
1938 Walt Disney's Mickey Mouse in Wonderland ..................80.00
1938 Ferdinand the Bull Cut-outs ................................70.00
1938 Snow White & the 7 Dwarfs Paint Book .......................65.00
1938 Snow White (linen-like) ....................................25.00
1938 Mickey Mouse in Numberland .................................85.00
1938 Walt Disney's Paint Book – Animals From Snow White ....25.00
1938 Walt Disney's Brave Little Taylor Paint & Crayon Book ....35.00
1938 Edgar Bergen's Charlie McCarthy Meets
         Walt Disney's Snow White ...............................25.00
1938 Walt Disney's Famous Seven Dwarfs ..........................25.00
1938 Toby Tortoise and the Hare (linenlike) ...................100.00
1938 Walt Disney's Elmer the Elephant (linen-like) ...........100.00
1938 Story of Mickey Mouse ......................................35.00
1938 Story of Minnie Mouse ......................................35.00
1938 Story of Pluto the Pup .....................................35.00
1938 Story of Clarabelle the Cow ................................30.00
1938 Story of Dippy the Goof ....................................30.00
1938 Walt Disney's Famous Seven Dwarfs ..........................25.00
1939 Mother Pluto ...............................................30.00
1939 Donald's Lucky Day .........................................70.00
1939 The Brave Little Tailor ....................................45.00
1939 Walt Disney's Pinocchio ....................................45.00
1939 The Farmyard Symphony ......................................35.00
1939 The Practical Pig ..........................................25.00
1940 Walt Disney's Fantasia Paint Book ..........................60.00
1940 Jiminy Cricket – A Story Paint Book ........................18.00
1940 Geppetto – A Story Paint Book ..............................15 .00
1940 Walt Disney's Dumbo Song Book ..............................20.00
1940 Walt Disney's Pinocchio (hardcover) ........................23.00
1941 Dumbo the Flying Elephant ..................................25.00
1942 Bambi Story Book ...........................................25.00
1943 Mickey's Dog Pluto – All Pictures Comic ....................25.00
1944 Donald Duck Is Here Again – All Pictures Comic .............25.00
1945 Funny Stories About Donald & Mickey ........................20.00
1946 Walt Disney's Mickey Mouse Paint Book ......................25.00
1948 Mickey Mouse in the Miracle Worker .........................20.00
1948 Walt Disney's Poor Pluto ...................................20.00
1948 Donald Duck and His Cat Troubles ...........................20.00
1948 Walt Disney's Mickey Mouse and the Boy Thursday ...........20.00
1948 Mickey and the Beanstalk ...................................20.00
1948 Walt Disney's Bongo ........................................15.00
1948 Donald Duck & The Boys .....................................20.00
1949 Donald Duck in the Great Kite Maker ........................20.00
1949 Walt Disney's Three Orphaned Kittens .......................15.00
1950 Cinderella .................................................15.00
1950 Walt Disney's Cinderella Paint Book ........................20.00
1951 Alice in Wonderland Punchout Book ..........................75.00
1951 Alice in Wonderland Paint Book .............................20.00
1952 Donald Duck & the Wishing Star .............................20.00
1952 Walt Disney's Peter Pan ....................................18.00
1952 Walt Disney's Whitman Story Book Goofy Dots ................20.00
1954 Walt Disney's Stormy .......................................10.00
1954 Donald Duck and Chip 'n Dale ...............................15.00
1954 Walt Disney's Donald Duck Dots .............................18.00
1954 Lady .......................................................12.00
1955 Walt Disney's Uncle Scrooge ................................20.00
1955 Walt Disney's Mickey Mouse Club –
         Old MacDonald Has a Farm ...............................15.00
1955 Donald Duck in Help Wanted .................................20.00
1956 Walt Disney's Spin & Marty .................................12.00

1956 Donald Duck and the New Bird House .........................12.00
1956 Donald Duck & the New Birdhouse ............................12.00
1957 Donald Duck in Frontierland ................................12.00
1957 Walt Disney's Mouseketeer Cut-outs .........................20.00
1957 Disneyland U.S.A. Coloring Book ............................20.00
1958 Walt Disney's Zorro Coloring Book ..........................15.00
1958 Walt Disney's Mouseketeer Linda Cut-Outs ...................15.00
1959 Sleeping Beauty ............................................12.00
1959 Walt Disney's Fairy Tale Coloring Book .....................20.00
1960 101 Dalmatians – Favorite Scenes to Set Up .................18.00
1960 Walt Disney's Kidnapped .....................................8.00
1962 Walt Disney's Goofy Coloring Book ..........................8.00
1962 Walt Disney's Wonderful World of Color,
         Color by Number Pictures ...............................20.00
1963 Annette & the Mystery of Smuggler's Cove ...................12.00
1964 Hayley Mills "The Moon Spinner" Cut Out Dolls ..............20.00
1964 Walt Disney's Disneyland ...................................20.00
1965 Hayley Mills "That Darn Cat" Wardrobe ......................20.00
1965 Winnie the Pooh .............................................7.00
1967 The Jungle Book .............................................7.00
1970 Walt Disney's Disneyland Coloring Book .....................10.00
1971 Bedknobs & Broomsticks .....................................10.00
1973 Walt Disney's Mary Poppins Paper Doll Book .................15.00
1977 Pete's Dragon ...............................................8.00
1977 The Rescuers ................................................8.00

### David McKay

1931 Mickey Mouse Storybook (softcover) .........................75.00
1931 Mickey Mouse Illustrated Movie Stories ....................175.00
1931 The Adventures of Mickey Mouse Book .......................170.00
1933 Who's Afraid of the Big Bad Wolf ...........................75.00
1934 Mickey Mouse Stories Book 2 ...............................140.00
1934 Peculiar Penguins From a Walt Disney Symphony .............45.00
1934 Mickey Mouse in Giantland ..................................75.00
1934 Mickey Mouse Movie Stories Book 2 .........................210.00
1936 Mickey Mouse and His Horse Tanglefoot .....................125.00
1937 Walt Disney's – The Country Cousin .........................65.00
1937 Walt Disney's Hiawatha .....................................40.00
1937 Snow White & the Seven Dwarfs .............................50.00

### Simon & Schuster

1947 Peter and the Wolf ..........................................8.00
1947 Dumbo .......................................................8.00
1948 Bongo .......................................................5.00
1950 So Dear to My Heart ........................................12.00
1950 Walt Disney's Once Upon a Winter Time ......................10.00
1950 Walt Disney's Cinderella's Friends .........................18.00
1952 Snow White & 7 Dwarfs ......................................22.00
1952 Walt Disney's Mother Goose .................................20.00
1953 Lady and the Tramp .........................................20.00
1955 Walt Disney's Davy Crockett ................................12.00
1955 Walt Disney's Robin Hood ...................................10.00
1955 Robin Hood Stamp Book ......................................15.00
1956 Walt Disney's Westward Ho the Wagons .......................18.00
1956 Our Friend the Atom ........................................18.00
1958 Walt Disney's Andy Burnett .................................15.00
1958 The Adventures of Zorro ....................................15.00
1981 Walt Disney's Snow White & 7 Dwarfs Pop Up .................8.00

### Blue Ribbon Books

1933 Three Little Pigs (hardcover) ..............................55.00
1933 Mickey Mouse in King Arthur's Court
         w/pop-up illustrations .................................375.00

1933 Minnie Mouse Pop-Up Book ..............................225.00

### Dean & Son (London)

1935 Mickey Mouse Movie Stories ....................375.00
1939 Walt Disney's Snow White Annual ....................150.00
1940 Walt Disney's Pinocchio ....................100.00
1947 Mickey Mouse Annual ....................25.00

### Simon & Schuster
### (Little Golden Books)

Listed in no particular date sequence based on continuous reissues of same titles.

Mickey Mouse Goes Christmas Shopping ....................10.00
Mickey Mouse & Pluto the Pup ....................10.00
Mickey Mouse's Picnic ....................10.00
Mickey Flies the Christmas Mail ....................8.00
Mickey Mouse & the Missing Mouseketeers ....................8.00
Surprise for Mickey Mouse ....................8.00
Mickey Mouse & His Space Ship ....................8.00
Mickey Mouse and the Great Lot Plot ....................5.00
Mickey Mouse The Kitten-Sitters ....................5.00
Mickey Mouse and the Best Neighbor Contest ....................5.00
Mickey Mouse & the Mouseketeers Ghost Town Adventure ....................5.00
Mickey Mouse & Goofy: The Great Bear Scare ....................5.00
Pluto Pup Goes to Sea ....................8.00
Donald's Duck Adventure ....................10.00
Donald Duck's Toy Train ....................10.00
Donald Duck & Santa Claus ....................10.00
Donald Duck & the Witch ....................10.00
Donald Duck's Christmas Tree ....................10.00
Donald Duck's Toy Sailboat ....................10.00
Donald Duck's Safety Book ....................10.00
Donald Duck in Disneyland ....................8.00
Donald Duck Prizedriver ....................8.00
Donald Duck & the Mouseketeers ....................8.00
Donald Duck & the Christmas Carol ....................8.00
Donald Duck Lost & Found ....................8.00
Donald Duck in Disneyland ....................8.00
Disneyland Parade with Donald Duck ....................8.00
Donald Duck & the Witch Next Door ....................5.00
Donald Duck in America on Parade ....................5.00
Donald Duck Private Eye ....................8.00
Donald Duck & the One Bear ....................5.00
Donald Duck; Instant Millionaire ....................5.00
Dumbo ....................10.00
Snow White and the Seven Dwarfs ....................10.00
Bambi ....................10.00
Pinocchio ....................10.00
Cinderella's Friends ....................8.00
Alice in Wonderland Meets the White Rabbit ....................8.00
Alice in Wonderland Finds the Garden of Live Flowers ....................8.00
Mad Hatter's Tea Party ....................8.00
Peter Pan and Wendy ....................8.00
Peter Pan and the Indians ....................8.00
Seven Dwarfs Find a House ....................8.00
Snow White and the Seven Dwarfs ....................8.00
Sleeping Beauty and the Good Fairies ....................10.00
Bongo ....................10.00
The Three Little Pigs ....................8.00
Ludwig Von Drake ....................8.00
Pinocchio and the Whale ....................8.00
Mary Poppins a Jolly Holiday ....................8.00

Mary Poppins ....................8.00
Winnie the Pooh: The Honey Tree ....................5.00
Winnie the Pooh Meets Gopher ....................5.00
Winnie the Pooh and Tigger ....................5.00
Thumper ....................5.00
Robin Hood ....................5.00
Robin Hood and the Daring Mouse ....................5.00
Through the Picture Frame (#1) ....................35.00
Cold Blooded Penguin (#2) ....................35.00
Peter & the Wolf ....................10.00
Uncle Remus ....................10.00
Johnny Appleseed ....................10.00
Once Upon a Wintertime ....................10.00
Santa's Toy Shop ....................8.00
Grandpa Bunny ....................8.00
Ugly Duckling ....................8.00
Mother Goose ....................8.00
Ben and Me ....................8.00
Chip 'N Dale at the Zoo ....................8.00
Lady ....................8.00
Disneyland on the Air ....................8.00
Little Man of Disneyland ....................8.00
Davy Crockett's Keelboat Race ....................8.00
Robin Hood ....................8.00
Jiminy Cricket, Fire Fighter ....................8.00
Goofy Movie Star ....................8.00
Mother Goose ....................8.00
The Shaggy Dog ....................10.00
Perri ....................8.00
Peter & the Wolf ....................5.00
Sleeping Beauty ....................5.00
Paul Revere ....................5.00
Old Yeller ....................5.00
Zorro ....................8.00
Zorro & the Secret Plan ....................5.00
Manni, the Donkey in the Forest World ....................8.00
Favorite Nursery Tales ....................5.00
Tonka ....................8.00
Darby O'Gill and the Little People ....................8.00
Goliath II ....................8.00
Uncle Remus ....................8.00
Toby Tyler ....................8.00
Lucky Puppy ....................8.00
Pollyanna ....................8.00
Bedknobs & Broomsticks ....................8.00
Swiss Family Robinson ....................8.00
The Flying Car ....................8.00
Babes in Toyland ....................10.00
The Toy Soldiers ....................10.00
Big Red ....................10.00
Lady ....................5.00
Savage Sam ....................5.00
The Sword in the Stone ....................8.00
The Wizard's Duel ....................8.00
Bunny Book ....................5.00
The Ugly Dachshund ....................5.00
The Jungle Book ....................5.00
The Aristocats ....................5.00
The Love Bug: Herbie's Special Friend ....................5.00
The Rescuers ....................5.00
Pete's Dragon ....................5.00

### Paper Items

Mickey Mouse Composition Booklet ............................. 85.00
Mickey Mouse Scrap Book Order Cards ........................ 20.00
Dental Appointment Card ........................................... 15.00
"There's Only One Blue Sunoco" ink blotter ................ 25.00
Post Cereal Box, cardboard, 1934 ............................. 120.00
United States Treasury/War Finance Committee Certificate ...... 50.00
Mickey Mouse Club – Mouseketeer Certificate, 1960's ............. 15.00
Donald Sunoco Ink Blotter, 1940's ............................. 20.00
Disney Character Seed Packets, 1977 .......................... 15.00
Mickey Mouse Club Card & Certificate, 1950's ............ 12.00
Walt Disney's Autograph ........................................... 325.00
Studio Issued Christmas Cards
    Fantasyland Castle, 1959 .................................. 75.00
    101 Dalmatians, 1960 ...................................... 70.00
    Disneyland, 1962 ............................................. 70.00
    Mickey with Hatchet, 1967 ............................... 70.00
RCA Victor Premium Placemats, 1961 ........................ 20.00
"Der Fuehrer's Face" Sheet Music .............................. 30.00
Hallmark Get-Well Cards, 1940's ............................... 20.00
Dopey Animated Valentine, 1938 ............................... 22.00
Disney Studio Menu, 1958 ......................................... 65.00
Movie Window Cards
    Babes in Toyland 1961 ..................................... 18.00
    Darby O'Gill & the Little People, 1959 ............... 20.00
    Moon Pilot, 1962 ............................................. 18.00
    Wheaties Premium Comic, 1950's ..................... 10.00
    Cheerios Premium Comic, 1940's ...................... 15.00

Snow White Lobby Card, original release .................... 200.00
D-X Dumbo Club Member's Card ................................ 20.00
Store Sign "Mickey Mouse Cookies" .......................... 175.00
Mickey Mouse Map of the United States, 1938, Dixon ........ 50.00
Walt Disney Pinocchio Poster Stamps, set of 32, 1940 ...... 50.00
Pinocchio Mechanical Valentine, 1939 ....................... 40.00
Christmas Package Decorations, 1930's ...................... 35.00
Mickey Mouse Birthday Party, Sheet Music, 1936 ........ 30.00
Disney World Pre-Construction Publicity Book, 1967 .... 20.00
Dumbo Pays Card, handed out at Disneyland, 1971 ...... 25.00
Mickey Mouse Picture Card Album (gum cards) ........... 75.00
Mickey Mouse with the Movie Stars Gum Cards
    Card #97 Ed Wynn ........................................... 60.00
    Card #102 Constance Bennett ........................... 55.00
    Card #103 Eddie Cantor .................................... 55.00
    Card #117 Wallace Beery ................................... 55.00
Large Size Mickey Mouse Bread Recipe Cards
    You Got to Get Up ............................................ 15.00
    Now Watch Me Pluto ........................................ 15.00
    Wanted A Horse ............................................... 15.00
Advertising Ink Blotter, 1930's .................................. 20.00
English Post Card ..................................................... 35.00
Mickey & the Beanstalk Birthday Card, 1940's ........... 20.00
Good Housekeeping Magazine Pages ........................... 15.00
Campbell's Pork and Beans Premium, 1950's .............. 25.00

# Schroeder's Antiques Price Guide

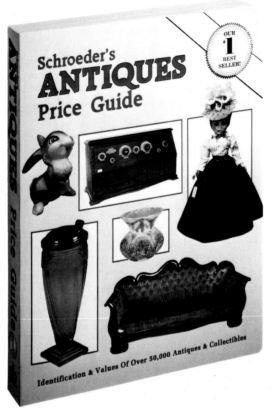

Schroeder's Antiques Price Guide has become THE household name in the antiques & collectibles field. Our team of editors work year-round with more than 200 contributors to bring you our #1 best-selling book on antiques & collectibles.

With more than 50,000 items identified & priced, Schroeder's is a must for the collector & dealer alike. If it merits the interest of today's collector, you'll find it in Schroeder's. Each subject is represented with histories and background information. In addition, hundreds of sharp original photos are used each year to illustrate not only the rare and unusual, but the everyday "fun-type" collectibles as well — not postage stamp pictures, but large close-up shots that show important details clearly.

Our editors compile a new book each year. Never do we merely change prices. Accuracy is our primary aim. Prices are gathered over the entire year previous to publication, from ads and personal contacts. Then each category is thoroughly checked to spot inconsistencies, listings that may not be entirely reflective of actual market dealings, and lines too vague to be of merit. Only the best of the lot remains for publication. You'll find Schroeder's Antiques Price Guide the one to buy for factual information and quality.

No dealer, collector or investor can afford not to own this book. It is available from your favorite bookseller or antiques dealer at the low price of $12.95. If you are unable to find this price guide in your area, it's available from Collector Books, P.O. Box 3009, Paducah, KY 42002-3009 at $12.95 plus $2.00 for postage and handling.

**8½ x 11", 608 Pages**                                                                       **$12.95**

**COLLECTOR BOOKS**

*A Division of Schroeder Publishing Co., Inc.*